Also from Westphalia Press
westphaliapress.org

Some African Highways

Westphalia Press
An imprint of Policy Studies Organization
1527 New Hampshire Ave., NW
Washington, D.C. 20036
info@ipsonet.org

ISBN-13: 978-1-63391-723-1
ISBN-10: 1-63391-723-1

Cover design by Jeffrey Barnes:
jbarnesbook.design

Daniel Gutierrez-Sandoval, Executive Director
PSO and Westphalia Press

Updated material and comments on this edition
can be found at the Westphalia Press website:
www.westphaliapress.org

Some African Highways

A Journey of Two American Women to Uganda and the Transvaal

by Caroline Kirkland

with an Intoduction by
Lieutenant-General Baden-Powell

WESTPHALIA PRESS
An imprint of Policy Studies Organization

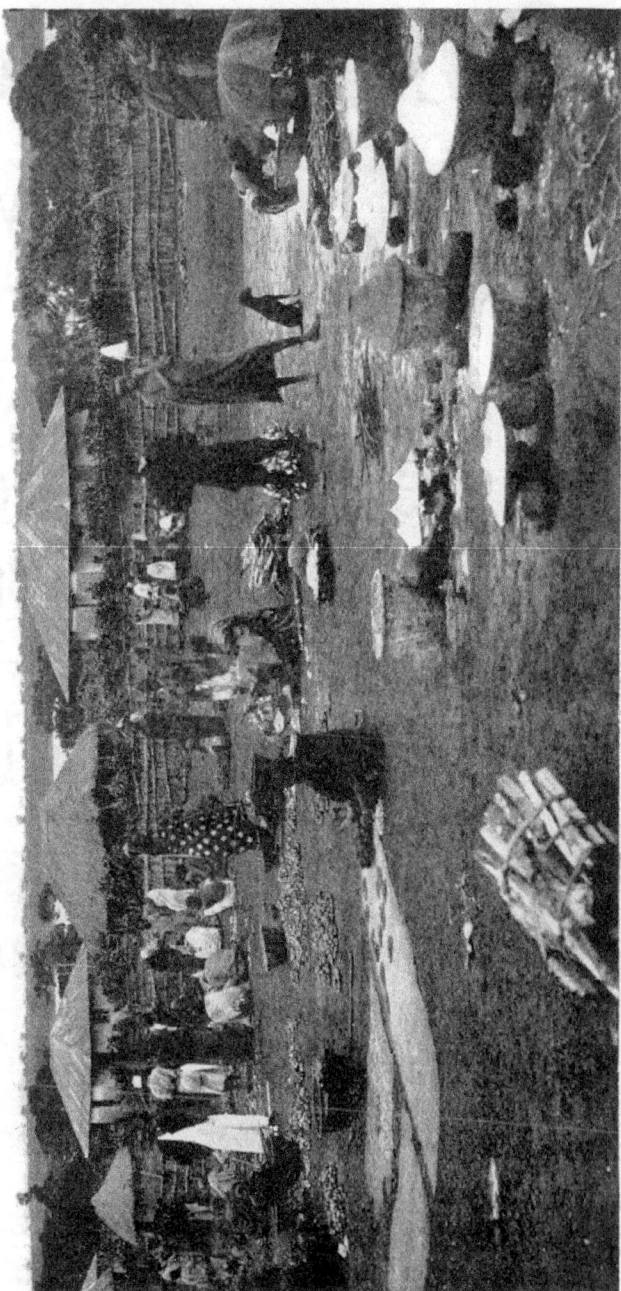

Market-Place at Entebbe

Some African Highways

COLONIAL PRESS
Electrotyped and Printed by C. H. Simonds & Co.
Boston, U.S.A.

SOME AFRICAN HIGHWAYS

A JOURNEY OF TWO AMERICAN WOMEN TO UGANDA AND THE TRANSVAAL

BY

CAROLINE KIRKLAND

With an Introduction by

LIEUTENANT-GENERAL BADEN-POWELL

With Illustrations from Photographs and a Map

BOSTON

DANA ESTES & COMPANY

PUBLISHERS

DEDICATED
TO MY MOTHER
THE BEST OF FELLOW
TRAVELLERS

Preface

————◆————

MUCH of the material in this volume first appeared in the *Chicago Tribune* in 1906. I have, however, added a good deal of new matter. I have taken especial pains to bring the chapter on Sleeping-sickness up to date, with the help of official reports furnished me by authorities in that part of Africa where this terrible scourge prevails.

This narrative is, however, merely a description of a trip made by two American women to Uganda and the Transvaal. It is published with the hope of interesting other Americans in one of the most fascinating and unique tours in the world — a tour which can be made with entire safety and great comfort. Where else can you look out from railway carriage windows and see zebras, gnus, giraffes, hyenas and even lions as you steam through

PREFACE

a land? Where else will you see utter savagery and the intricate ceremony of modern social life in close contact? Where else will you see such contrasting methods side by side as you see here in Africa where English, French, Germans, Italians, Belgians and Portuguese are addressing the same problems in their different ways? And what other great continent can you circumnavigate in ease and comfort and security?

To the lover of strong contrasts, of high lights and black shadows, of wonderful scenery, of great spaces, of all that is new and free and stirring, I recommend a trip to this dark, mysterious, violent and enchanting country. We two women only touched the surface of it, but we were ever conscious of much that we could not see, nor hear, nor formulate, but which exists in a land teeming with fierce and savage life.

CAROLINE KIRKLAND.

Foreword

———◆———

HOW I should like to be a woman! It must be nice to lie back in your cushions and watch the men doing things which they think very clever, knowing all the time that you can do them very much better yourself if you only care to try.

For instance: I am convinced that if women were to take up the art of scouting they would easily beat men at the game.

They have a greater natural gift of observation and a most uncannily clever knack of "putting this and that together" and then deducing meaning from the smallest signs.

Hence it comes that when women travel into the lesser-known countries of the world, as they frequently do nowadays, they bring this power of observation into play with remarkable results. And of all women in the world

FOREWORD

I would place our American cousins at the top of the list for this particular quality.

Unfortunately it is only too seldom that they record their impressions, but when they do their pages ripple with little touches both quaint and human which are the direct result of quick observation and which go to paint the character of countries and people far more vividly than the more erudite writings of the mere man who plods along basing his remarks very largely on what he has already read or been told of the country now spread out before him.

East Africa has only of recent years come within the range of civilized travel, and is still a land of romantic suggestion as well as of future interest, with an atmosphere of piracy and slave-trade still haunting its palm-grown coral inlets, where grave old Arab merchants roll in wealth derived from ivory both of the black as well as white variety. Here still you see barbaric tribes of naked warriors ready for blood with their war-songs and weapons. And you may yet " snap " the prehistoric rhinoceros on the same quarter-plate with a mighty modern locomotive on the Uganda line. Here too you can watch the Western white-clad pioneer at his work of pushing back the jungle to give room for future fields of commerce.

These and many more are things which have, it is true, been written about already by men connected with those parts, but in the present volume a lady-scout has taken them in hand from a different and less tedious point of view.

Having been over much of the ground one-self one can only envy the quick perception and accuracy of touch with which Miss Caroline Kirkland has, in few words, so faithfully sketched the minor points which go to make these lands the fascinating fields they are to all who visit them.

R. S. S. BADEN - POWELL,
Lieut. - Gen'l.

Contents

List of Illustrations

LIST OF ILLUSTRATIONS

VICTORIA NYANZA

SPEKE GULF

Ihangiro

Kyimoani

Bukoma

Wana-Muëri

Bukhosa

Butundwe

Usambiro

Uyofu

Utumbara

Usonga

Ugomba

Watu

Ubagwa

Wakwande

Ukumbu

Mango ye

Usanda

Warendo

Uhanga

Usmawo

Urui

Ulutwa

Miatu

Washashi

Kiniamong

Ikiy

Some African Highways

CHAPTER I

HISTORICAL SKETCH OF EAST AFRICA AND UGANDA

SAID Solomon of old: " There is no remembrance of former things; neither shall there be any remembrance of things that are to come with those that shall come after." So, from the time of Homer down to the middle of the last century, the sources of the Nile have been discovered and lost, and rediscovered and lost again with each new era of enlightenment. Speke, in 1858, had the same thrill on his first sight of the great lake, which now is known as Victoria Nyanza, as the original discoverer who wrote his book, probably on papyrus, either in Greek or Phoenician. He, that Greek or Phoenician, together with his

writings and maps, has long since, with those
that came after, treading unknowing in his
footsteps, disappeared in that vast darkness
which envelops and absorbs all human endeavor. Mr. Stanley, however, in his invaluable work, " In Darkest Africa," gives a curious
and noteworthy collection of maps from ancient
times down to his own in which the Nile is
traced to its sources, all including various dis-
tortions of the great interior African lakes,
and of those contributing factors, the classic
mountains of the moon.

Speke's first view of the Victoria Nyanza
was from the southern shores. He was then
exploring in a subordinate capacity, having
left his superior, Richard Burton, ill of a variety of African maladies, many days' journey
to the south. The story of Speke's subsequent
return to England, and of his claiming and
wearing the laurels for his discovery is too well
known to bear repetition here. Four years
later he came back with Grant, and by a devious
approach, via the south end and west shore
of the lake, made his way to the capital of

Uganda, Mengo (now generally known as Kampala). The then King of Uganda, M'tesa, sent him to the north outlet of the lake, where these two explorers were the first modern white men to see that great initial swirl of the Nile over the lip of the lake, as the famous river starts on its way northward. They named this drop the Falls of Ripon, though it can hardly be considered as more than a cataract. The native name for the river was Kivira, while the lake was called Ukéréwé.

It was a lucky leap in the dark on the part of Speke and Grant to say that this was the real beginning of the Nile. They did little to verify their theory, but subsequent discoveries proved them right, and so they get the credit for it. They, and all those early explorers, however, deserve much praise and respect for the dangers, trials, and discomforts which they met and overcame. The footsteps which they made with such pains and labor in the jungles and forests, and on the plains of tropical Africa, have since been trodden down and out by so many other adventurous explorers of diverse nationalities that the road has become a broad highway, with well equipped trains and steamers to convey an ever-increasing throng to those once forbidding and inaccessible regions.

Because we have not a continuous record in European languages of the vast territory of East and Central Africa does not mean that it has not had a progressing history. It is far older in obtainable chronicle than either of the American continents. The navigators of ancient times came in their galleys down this East Coast. Solomon's mines are by common consent placed in this region. While his illustrious guest, the Queen of Sheba, is supposed by many to have come from this same part of the world to do him homage.

For centuries the Arabs have controlled the fortunes and trade of this enormously rich territory. The influences of their language, customs, and traditions are to-day to be observed on every hand in studying the natives of East Africa.

The principal tribe there are the Swahilis, descendants of Arabs, Persians and Africans.

Namirembe Cathedral (Protestant) Uganda

Ripon Falls, from Usoga Side

The very name is from the Arab " sahel," meaning " of the coast." The language of these Swahilis is the common intermediary speech of the natives from Zanzibar to Uganda — though each tribe has its own tongue. The Arabs have done much to plant and foster Mohammedanism in North and Central Africa. According to reports from the Christian missions the converts to Christianity far outnumber the converts to Mohammedanism. I have not seen the reports from the Arabs. If a tree is to be judged by its fruit, however, I should say that the latter form of religion evolves as decent an African as the former. To a certain limited degree the teachings of Mahomet are better adapted to that extremely elementary creature, the African native, than is our more abstract and ethical faith. A religion of many forms and ceremonies, which also includes much ablution, and a total abstaining from alcoholic beverages, and which permits a plurality of wives, fits excellently certain conditions of a tropical climate and a savage people.

The Christian missions, Catholic and Protestant, have, however, done a great work in East and Central Africa. Their converts number two hundred thousand, and at their headquarters in Kampala churches, schools, and various industries testify to their excellent work. The principal Protestant organization is The Church Missionary Society, which has been for many years under the administration of Bishop Tucker; while the Roman Catholic Church is represented by the White Fathers (a French mission with headquarters in Algiers), and the Mill Hill Fathers, an offshoot of an organization of the same name in England.

The introduction of Christian missionaries into this part of Africa is connected with a curious tragedy worth recording here. When, in 1875, Stanley reached Uganda, he found M'tesa, the king, pondering the question of a desirable religion for his people. Stanley's presentment of the doctrines of christianity impressed M'tesa profoundly. Just at that moment a messenger from General Gordon, who had been sent to investigate Uganda to see whether it was a desirable territory to annex, appeared at Mengo. This was a Belgian, one Linant de Bellefonds. By him Stanley sent his famous letter to the *Daily Telegraph* urging English missionaries to start on the conversion of Uganda. The unfortunate Belgian was set upon by the Bari tribe on his return journey to Khartoum and was killed in the neighborhood of Gondokoro. His body was found by a punitive expedition sent out by the government, and on removing the long knee-boots he wore at the time of his death Stanley's letter was found where de Bellefonds had tucked it — probably at the moment of attack. The blood-stained missive was forwarded to its destination with an explanation of its adventures and delays, and its publication brought immediate answer. In less than a year the Anglican missionaries of the Church Missionary Society had started in two divisions — one via the Nile and one via the East Coast — for Uganda.

In 1879 the White Fathers also established themselves in that country, and have now a great and flourishing institution which has branches all over Uganda.

To return to the history of this region: when in 1480 Vasco da Gama circumnavigated Africa he sailed into the harbor of Mombasa, then known as Mvita, an Arab and African settlement. Narrowly escaping disaster on the cruel reefs that menace the entrance of this harbor, he found on drifting into the port, a charming inland shelter where, as they still do to-day, tranquil waters lapped white coral sands shaded by groves of rustling palms. Doubtless before this Mombasa, or Mvita, had seen much bloodshed and strife. Certainly after this the town did.

In 1500 the Portuguese returned and took it by storm. It was retaken later by the Arabs and changed hands in violence fifteen times down to the early part of the nineteenth century. Its position and harbors made it the most important port after Zanzibar on the whole East Coast.

In 1827 it fell into the hands of the Sultan of Zanzibar. From that time its prestige and importance diminished until the beginning of this century, when a new, strong lease of life was given to it by making it the coast terminus of the wonderful Uganda Railway.

The old Portuguese fort, built in 1594, and restored in 1635, is one of the principal landmarks of the town, and after its centuries of many strife is now not unfitly used by the English as a prison. On its turreted battlements turbaned Sihks from India do sentinel duty to-day, and their chief occupation seems to be to watch the tennis played daily by the British residents on the glaring clay courts under those frowning, windowless walls.

The town is situated on an island three miles long, one and a half miles broad, whose greatest altitude is only seventy feet above the encircling sea. On the west it is connected with the mainland by a causeway. Its two harbors, one to the northeast and a deeper one to the southwest, make it a fine port for vessels of varying size. The largest steamers unload in the latter haven at a settlement called Kilindini. A winding, well-buoyed channel leads to it.

SOME AFRICAN HIGHWAYS

There is much old Arab and Portuguese architecture in the narrow twisting streets of the town. Camoens, who spent some time here before going to India in the fifteenth century, sings of its "noble edifices fairly planned on the seaboard." It exports from the neighboring mainland sugar cane, tobacco, hides, rubber, sesame, copra, chilis, and other tropical products. It is the chief entrance to the vast territory known as British East Africa.

From the "Handbook of British East Africa," published in 1892 by the Intelligence Division of the English War Office, I will endeavor to give an idea of the boundaries of this territory, also a slight suggestion as to its configuration and its inhabitants. Since the publication of this handbook Uganda has been separated from the administration of British East Africa and has been given a commissioner (or governor) and a judiciary of its own. But this is merely an internal difference. It does not affect the outlines of the English holdings in Central and East Africa. These possessions include the islands of Zanzibar and Pemba and on the mainland a stretch of four hundred miles of coast between the rivers Juba on the north, and Umba on the south. With this coast, as the basic line, the territory spreads out to the northwest, including 900 miles on the equator, an east and west measurement of course; while its greatest breadth north and south is seven hundred and fifty miles on the 39th meridian. Its area is seven hundred thousand square miles. On the north the parallel of 6° north and the river Juba, from its intersection by that parallel to the sea, separate it from Italian Africa. On the south it is divided from German East Africa by a line drawn along the parallel of 1° south latitude from Congo Free State to the east coast of Victoria Nyanza and thence to the mouth of the Umba on the coast. This line is diverted to give Great Britain the Mfumbiro Mountain on the west and to Germany Mount Kilimanjaro on the east. The western boundary is limited by the Congo Free State, north of which it merges into the region above the Nile basin formerly part of the dominions of Egypt, now known as the Soudan. This part eastward to Victoria Nyanza includes the Protectorate of Uganda, and it is the opinion of some (generally English officials in the Soudan) that Uganda should be included in the Soudan government. Various authorities, among whom is Sir Harry Johnston, think that one administration should be made of Uganda and British East Africa. Uganda officials do not look favorably on either amalgamation. Certain it is that it is likely to be only a short time before the northern outlet of Uganda via the Nile region will be more travelled and more serviceable to this potentially rich country than its present eastern outlet.

A step in this direction was the opening in 1906 of Port Sudan on the Red Sea. While the Cape to Cairo Railway is daily pushing up from the south and down from the north, and will before long meet in Uganda, completing this gigantic and wonderfully interesting achievement.

But " this is another story." Great Britain

24

has, with her usual acumen, got the choice morsels in the subdivision of Africa among the European powers. British East Africa is a plateau rising gradually from the Indian Ocean. Its ordinary level in the interior varies from three thousand to six thousand feet above the sea. A curious feature of this vast plateau is the existence of detached, quite unrelated mountain masses rising from it. " These are of enormous dimension, both in height and area," says the Handbook.

Mounts Kenia and Kilimanjaro lie between the lake and the sea and both rise eighteen thousand feet above the sea. They are two hundred miles apart and in clear weather both are visible from the Uganda Railway; Kilimanjaro the first day and Mount Kenia the second. The latter is plainly an extinct volcano, having the unmistakable conformation of the world's chimneys.

West and somewhat north of Lake Victoria Ruwenzori, nearly twenty thousand feet in height, veils its massive head for three hundred days a year in impenetrable fogs. The effect when it does burst forth must, to judge from Stanley's account of it, be one of the great spectacles of the earth. Its flanks, clothed in the lower parts with dense tropical forests, rise gradually to stupendous peaks and snow fields of enormous sweep, which probably gained for it the ancient and classical name of Mountains of the Moon.

One hundred miles south rises the volcanic shape of Mfumbiro to over fourteen thousand feet, and to the north of the lake Mount Elgon towers to a similar height.

Besides these detached mountains, each of which rises like a monarch from the African plateau, there are mountain ranges running north and south and attaining a height of ten thousand feet.

One of the most curious of the geographic phenomena which individualize Africa is a gigantic gash in the earth's crust that runs along meridian 36° east for some seven hundred miles from latitude 4° south to 6° north. Where the Uganda Railway crosses this the west lip is known as the Nandi Escarpment, and as the train zigzags swiftly down the face of the east lip, the Mau Escarpment, the scene in looking across the "Rift Valley," as it is called, is one of unforgettable splendor. But my impression of this effect comes later in this narrative. The floor of this depression varies from six thousand feet above the sea at Lake Elmenteita to fifteen hundred feet at Lake Rudolf. In it are many " self-contained " lakes, that is, not having outlet or inlet. Many of them are salt. In English territory are Lakes Elmenteita, Naivasha, Nakuro, and Baringa, and further north the great Lakes Rudolf and Stephanie.

From the east side of this rift the rivers flow into the Indian Ocean; while from the west they flow to Victoria Nyanza and thence, via the Nile, to the Mediterranean. The principal of the rivers flowing east are the Juba, mentioned' before and rising in the Abyssinian highlands, the Tana, rising under Mount Kenia, and the Sabaki, formed by the junction of the Athi and the Tsavo Rivers.

As the distance between the west lip of the

rift and Lake Victoria is not very great, no rivers of any notable size flow westward. But the waters of all the streams that drain that side eventually flow into the Nile and thence to the Mediterranean.

Sir Harry Johnston, in his excellent work, " The Uganda Protectorate," divides the natives of East and Central Africa into those descended from the Bantu stock (which is the chief origin for many varying tribes from the equator to the Cape) and the Nilotic tribes. The chief of the Nilotic tribes in East Africa are the Masai (a very superior race living east of the lake) and the Kavirondos, and many of the tribes living north and west of Uganda. Some authorities include the Baganda, or inhabitants of Uganda. Aside from the uniformity in speech, the descendants of the Nile tribes are distinguished by a simplicity of attire rivalling that of Adam and Eve before the fall. They may don skins or draperies for warmth or to be dressy, but never for decency. As the Baganda have always been quite the contrary and wear many and most classical

Kavirondo Warrior

Masai Women

draperies, and are most scrupulous in regard to decency, this makes a great gulf between them and their more primitive neighbors, to whom they are apt to refer in scorn as the *Ukedi* ("the naked"). Their speech and features both ally them, however, with the Nile negroes.

The Bantu stock is widespread and includes the natives of West and South Africa and many of the tribes of East and Central Africa, but its offshoots do not seem to be equal, either physically or mentally, to the descendants of the Nile negroes, although they far outnumber them.

There is among the natives in Uganda a system of land tenure which is carefully guarded by the English authorities. This makes it difficult for Great Britain to make big land grants similar to those which have been made in British East Africa to such great landholders as the British East Africa Company, or to such individuals as Lord Hindlip, Lord Delamere, and others.

Among the principal tribes living between

the Indian Ocean and Lake Victoria besides the Masai and Kavirondo, are the Kikuyu, the Nandis, the Wanyenwezi, the Suks, and the Turkanas. The generic term for these East African tribes is Wanyika.

North and west of the lake the Usoga, the Unyoro, Ankole, Toro, and Usongora tribes compose what is now known as the Kingdom of Uganda, but was formerly a great empire called Kittara. This also included the Ruanda and Karagwe people, who live beyond the present British frontiers.

The little King of Uganda, Daudi Chwa, now sits at Kampala, the native capital of the state, and holds nominal rule with a royal court, soldiers, and civil officials.

There is outward harmony, but that all is not as serene as it appears is manifested by little signs here and there, while the murder of Harry Galt, which is related later, is a serious manifestation of an inward tendency to revolt to which the English are somewhat oblivious. They are too apt to take it for granted that because they establish and maintain a better rule they are entirely acceptable to an alien and savage people. This belief in their superiority has before this led the English into trouble, which, with more insight and foresight, might have been avoided or minimized. They are courageous and just, but are apt to be over-confident.

The immediate predecessors of the present king were M'tesa, who welcomed the first white men in 1858 and was always friendly to them, and Mwanga, who succeeded him and nearly ruined his people by the gross immorality he introduced and fostered among them, and by his bloody ferocity.

The chronicles of his doings make grewsome reading in the writings of the travellers of that part of Africa in the last quarter of the nineteenth century. Among his crimes is the historic murder of Bishop Hannington in 1886.

The great moment in the history of East Africa and Uganda came when the Uganda Railway, begun in 1896, was completed and opened for traffic in 1903. Then indeed was that part of the Dark Continent flooded with light. Of this as an engineering feat I am not competent to write, except to call attention to that part of the route when the train drops down the eastern lip to the floor of the great Rift Valley in an incredibly short space of time, which cannot fail to impress the veriest tyro in railway engineering. But from the point of view of the tourist I can say that it is probably the most wonderful and interesting railway journey in the world. Where else can you look from the car windows and see herds of zebras, gnus, and gazelles of many kinds grazing within easy gunshot? Where else can you behold wild ostriches teetering across the plains, and giraffes *aux naturelles* awkwardly scampering away, or hyenas tearing undisturbed at carrion left by some beast of prey? Or where will your train be arrested to hunt a lion crouched in plain sight not seventy feet away? Or from what other car windows will you see a lioness and four cubs loping peacefully by the track? While in what other railway journey will you see so many types of savages as those which line the way from Mombasa to the lake, varying from the lightly clad coast tribes to the clay-plastered Kikuyus and the stark naked Kavirondos?

A fuller account of this wonderful trip comes in a later chapter, where I leave generalities and embark on the more personal narrative which is the main part of this book. My wish now is to give a slight idea of this wonderfully interesting country, so that some of my compatriots may have the inestimable delight of visiting these regions before the extraordinary panorama has changed; before the wild animals have retired to remote regions; before missionaries have clad the savages in custom-made trousers and petticoats; before Cook is escorting chattering flocks of New England schoolma'ams to the whilom lairs and jungles of fierce savagery.

Oh, you who have health and money and energy, hasten to see the great spectacle before the inevitable change comes!

CHAPTER II

THE wind blew hard the night before we
sailed from Naples on the *Prinzregent*
for Mombasa in British East Africa, in October,
1905, so we were not unprepared for the choppy
seas that met us in the bay, and broke against
the frowning cliffs of Capri as we ploughed
along under the ruins of Villa Jove. The breaking waves dashed high on the stern and rock-
bound coast of Calabria when we steamed
across the Gulf of Salerno. They beat against
the cliffs of lovely Amalfi and flung themselves
in great white legions on the more sloping
shores of Minori and Maori. The wind trailed
and twisted the low-lying clouds across the
face of the mountains and sent many of the
frailer passengers on the ship below.

When the shores quite disappeared in mist

we went to our cabin to arrange ourselves and our belongings in the contracted space that was to be our abode for the next sixteen days. We were fortunate in having one of the largest cabins on the ship, but even so it takes some ingenuity to adjust two women, three steamer trunks, and accompanying hampers and suit-cases to an accommodation measuring perhaps ten feet by fourteen. In a voyage on tropical seas one needs more clothes than in cooler climes. A frequent change of light frocks for women and linen or duck suits for men is necessary for comfort. And while it is possible to have laundry work done on almost any steamer making long, hot voyages, it is better to be independent of such work. There is never a *blanchisseuse de fin* on these boats, and clothes are hung to dry in an interior dark drying room, which, for some reason, seems usually to drip with iron rust, as demonstrated by the much spotted linen that emerges from the process. Furthermore, it is the pleasant and comfortable custom on these ships sailing tropical seas to dress for dinner in some frock or habit of a festive effect. Which means more changes, more luggage, and more room needed.

We (which " we " means my mother and myself) were taking down to my sister in Central Africa an Italian maid, a young girl from Capri, and here let me digress to say that for the kind of unexpected service required, for the vicissitudes of such a journey and the inconveniences and trials of life in those newly settled regions, an Italian girl, if you can get just the right one, is the best kind to take. She is not used to any comfort or luxury in her own country. She is, as a rule, adaptable, and if she be of that right kind specified, she will be amiable, docile, strong, and sympathetic. Nannina was all these and proved to be a treasure. Although she is in a far-away land, among a strange people, who do not speak her language, in a settlement where she is the only white servant, she has never complained or been anything but cheerful. I should say that it might be hard to find another like her had I not had a similar experience with a maid whom I took down to South Africa with me in 1899.

FROM NAPLES TO MOMBASA

Returning to the decks, we established ourselves in our long chairs and took a survey of our
fellow passengers. We found them to be about
half and half English and German — an un-
malleable lot, each looking askance at his
neighbor. Except for Countess von Goetzen,
the American-born wife of the governor of
German East Africa, my mother and I were
the only Americans on the ship.

The German passengers were generally officials, who with their families were returning
to their posts in German East Africa. Among
the English there was a greater variety of
object. Some were officials, some were people
who had taken up land out there in the wilderness of British East Africa, or had concessions
they were anxious to develop. Others were
after big game; while still others were officers
hurrying to their posts in the interior on account
of an outbreak of the warlike Nandis. As a
rule the passengers were an interesting gathering of people, with the commercial element,
so pronounced on the African West Coast
route and on the North Atlantic steamers,

strongly absent. When the strangeness of the first few days wore off the hours passed very pleasantly, and the evenings, after we reached the warmer southern seas, were especially charming. Men and women in evening dress sat about in gay groups on the decks taking their after-dinner coffee, while many of the women, following the English custom, joined the men in smoking cigarettes. In the brilliantly lighted saloon, whose windows opened on the deck, there would be music, while, later in the evening, tables, both indoors and out, would be set for cards or chess. And each night the air grew warmer and softer and the sea smoother. But this is anticipating.

When we first sailed from Naples, there was great uncertainty as to when we should get through the Suez canal. The English steamer, the *Chatham*, carrying dynamite, had been sunk in the channel some three weeks before to prevent its cargo blowing up the whole canal in a fire which occurred on the steamer. It had been partially dislodged, allowing one relay of ships to pass; but a second attempt to clear the channel had been made a few days previous to our sailing date, and the way was not yet open.

As we drew near Port Said we noticed an ominous absence of approaching steamers, so we were in a measure prepared for the news we received there that the canal was still closed. The outer and inner harbors were both filled with ships from all quarters of the globe, the accumulation of ten days of waiting. When we woke up on the morning after our arrival we found ourselves, nose out into the stream, aligned with a waiting host. Next us was a Russian ship, carrying back to Eastern Siberia the inhabitants who had been driven away by the war. The decks seemed crowded with women and children, who were evidently to restore domestic life to that devastated region.

Port Said is much improved since I was there in 1899, when it seemed the jumping-off place for the West and the East. It has a more law-abiding appearance now. Its main streets have some decent-looking hotels, while the shops, with their ostrich-feather fans and boas,

Maltese lace, Indian silver and ivory, and Chinese and Japanese curios, are quite alluring. The highways and byways are filled with specimens of many of the strange tribes of Africa and Asia, draped in all colors of the rainbow and varying in skin tint from the pale chocolate of some inland Arabs to the luminous black of the Nubians.

Those of the ship's passengers who were not already so provided bought here the indispensable pith helmet with which to fortify themselves against the deadly tropical sun. The especial point to be protected is the nape of the neck, the base of the brain. This properly sheltered, there is little danger to Europeans in the tropics, but there is still room for much discomfort.

As the canal was to be opened a day or so later, and as the ships carrying the mails were allowed precedence of all others, we, being of this class, moved up the line, passing our less fortunate neighbors, and took our place in the stately procession a few miles or so outside of Port Said. For a day we lay with the desert on

A Native Canoe — Uganda

Fish Traps, Victoria Nyanza

either side of us, though here it does not look like the desert, as vast tracts of shallow water menace the canal's banks.

An occasional camel loped along the road that runs by the canal; queer African cranes trailed across the sunset sky; and by the time a day and a night of silent waiting had passed we were once more on our way. It was a unique and memorable sight, the seventy-five or more steamers bearing the world's commerce gliding slowly down the narrow waterway. By day as far as one could see in either direction was a line of masts, spars, and funnels; by night to the rear was a glittering trail of the fierce bow-lights with which each ship illumines its way down the canal.

About midway we passed the wreckage of the *Chatham*, lying scattered over the adjacent sands, while the skeleton of its steel hull reared ugly, torn sides in the great hole in the canal's banks made by the explosion. Visions of distant, violet-tinted mountains hovered on the eastern horizon. Nearer at hand low, windowless mud huts, like ant-hills of a larger growth, marked an Arab settlement. Except for a slight ripple of the sluggish waters against the shelving sands of the shores, we should hardly have known that we were moving, so slow and silent was our progress.

We met the north-coming steamers in the Bitter Sea. I counted thirty ranged in a great semicircle. Another forty lay in the Gulf of Suez next morning when we hove to. Here our canal tax of nearly ten thousand dollars was paid, and one stage of our trip lay behind us.

The Red Sea in October is undeniably hot. But the decks were well shaded with canvas and one could sit with comparative comfort on the breezy side, where the passengers made little groups, reading or chattering or playing cards. At four in the afternoon we usually adjourned for tea or coffee in the dining-room, and later the gorgeous sunsets for which the Red Sea is famous flamed up on the western sky in palpitating splendor. After dinner came those charming evenings which I have already mentioned. I should like to have looked at the ship from the soft, thick encircling outer darkness. It must have made a brilliant picture as it glided southward under the glittering stars and through the still waters with its brightly lit decks thronged with gay people, while music floated out from its upper saloon, mingling with weird native chants from the lower regions of the ship.

Those who at night preferred the rather troubled slumber on the deck in long chairs to the soaking sleep in the cabins had the better part. For, after the lights were out and the eyes grew accustomed to the darkness, a soft permeating glow seemed to come from the stars and to fill the night with a faint glory. Shadowy, unrecognizable forms hovered about the decks until each passenger found his own couch, when came silence, and a refreshing peace seemed to rise from the cool cisterns of the midnight air. Dawn and the deck swabbers drove us down-stairs early.

Our next stop was at Asab, a dreary port in Abyssinia belonging to Italy, where we collected a strange lot of three hundred warriors from the desert, Nubians, Somalis, and Sou··

danese to fight a native uprising in German East Africa. A chattering, bizarre, insect-ridden batch they were! Their horrid Egyptian flies invaded the ship, crawling over everything and everybody. They seemed to have a fashion of creeping about the eyes of men and beasts. It took a day of brisk sea breezes to blow them away.

We spent four or five hot and glaring hours lying in the harbor at Asab, looking at its dreary, crumbling, low white buildings, crouched under a few tired-looking palms that only accentuated the utter lack of verdure, the ghastly barrenness of the place. The delay was caused by the preposterous port duties the Italian authorities at Asab wished to charge us — 1,800 lire. Ours was probably the only ship of any size which had ever put in at that port. After waiting some time for answers to cable messages sent home for instructions, our captain ordered up the anchor and we steamed away without paying any duties at all.

Our new passengers, the desert warriors, were very interesting to watch. There was a great diversity in the gorgeous colors of their draperies, in their types and customs. Their deck was daily turned into shambles as their native sheep, ill-shapen and ugly, were slaughtered according to the laws of Mahomet. At sunset, each on his prayer-rug, these followers of the Prophet turned toward Mecca with their evening salutations to Allah Illa Allah.

One evening they were allowed to have a dance. The rhythm of their repetitious tom-toms, the monotonous shuffling of their steps to time kept by hand-clapping, worked them up to a sort of strange frenzy. The music and manner of dancing resembled to a remarkable degree a dance of Crow Indians which I had seen in Wyoming the preceding year.

A horrible night at Aden, when, in sweltering heat, we lay coaling from midnight until six in the morning, left us exhausted. During the process of coaling the ship all ports and doors are closed. A fine black dust falls over the decks, while within a stifling atmosphere saps vitality.

The rounding of Capes Guardafui and Ras

Hafun — the two easternmost points of Africa — is a very difficult bit of seamanship. There is no lighthouse on any point of land; the shore is wild, rocky and inhabited by fierce savages; and the currents set strongly toward the land in many places, while the island of Abd al Kuri forbids a wide berth being given to these promontories. Every year more than one fine ship goes ashore to be sacked by the natives. Until lately short shrift was accorded to the survivors of the wrecks, but now the English government offers a money bonus for every life saved, and gives the ship and its cargo to the tribes. We passed not far from the wreck of a fine six thousand ton ship from China, belonging to a French line, which had been swept on this cruel coast some three months before. Her chart-house had been carried intact off the ship by the savages, and was now the home of the chief. With our glasses we could see it gleaming on a knoll. A Russian gunboat had saved the passengers and crew, the former arriving at Aden in their night attire, everything being lost in the wreck. The Italian government, which has control (nominal) of this part of Africa, cannot put up a lighthouse without first building a fort to protect its operations and to guard the light after it is built. A wild, forbidding, utterly barren point of land is this easternmost cape of the Dark Continent. As one sails away from it and looks back to it, the main promontory turns into a massive and splendid lion's head that appears to be looking eastward and brooding over the desolation of that particular corner of the earth.

The tail end of the monsoon, the great southerly trade-wind of the Indian Ocean, molested the calm of our last days before arriving at Mombasa; but only a day late we reached this port. It is, as recounted in my introductory chapter, an old Portuguese settlement, a relic of the era of Portugal's greatness as a sea power. It lies on a low island connected with the mainland by a long causeway. The harbor by the town being too shallow for our large ship, we glided by a well-buoyed channel around to the inner side of the island to Kilindini. As we entered this channel, to the right lay Mombasa with its low bungalows buried in foliage, the old Portuguese fort being a conspicuous landmark. To the left the waves broke in vast white semicircles on the coral reefs, while the adjoining point of land with its dense forest of palms presented a most tropical appearance. Robinson Crusoe might at any moment have come out of the jungle, and signalled us.

Being but a few miles off the equator, Mombasa does not invite to physical exertion, neither does the climate encourage horses, so the question of intramural transportation is solved by a system of hand-run trams, called trolleys. Narrow tracks lead from everybody's front door through every street. On these are run light little cars, consisting of two seats (back to back), with a sheltering hood. Two native boys push these from behind at a swift rate. In front is a foot-brake that can be operated by the person sitting on the left, in case of too great speed or danger of collision. At every corner or intersection are switches, so that one can go in any direction. The system is most complete and is eminently suited to conditions in Mombasa. Gharries or rickshaws supplement these, while one or two of the Hindoo merchants, who batten on East Africa, have carriages and horses.

A clamoring horde of African porters bore us and our luggage in long boats from the ship to the shore, where we clambered up a low, spongy bank and went to the customs office, a corrugated iron shed, not far away. The air reeked with that unmistakable smell of Africa, which is not all African humanity, but includes in some strange way the smell of the earth, the strong perfume of tropical flowers, the scent of sun shining hot on iron, of stones reluctantly exuding moisture at the same solar bidding. Once in the nostrils it never leaves you while you are on the Dark Continent.

Kindness and courtesy met us from the moment we landed. All further care seemed taken from us. An official of the Uganda Railway took us in his own trolleys the twenty minutes' trip to Mombasa. Mangoes, baobobs, and mimosa-trees shaded the way. Hibiscus and other brilliant blossoms glared at us from the shrubbery. Frangipani — which until now I thought was merely a name for a French perfume — scented the air from waxen blossoms, and everywhere was the softly chattering, brilliantly clad African race.

We were housed in a hotel of Africo-Portuguese architecture, where every step shook the whole structure. Each room opened by a high overhead grating into all the other contiguous apartments, an arrangement excellent for airiness but fatal to even the most primitive privacy. The bedchambers were furnished with the barest necessities, nor did the bedcovers encourage the hope that we were the first to woo slumber on those rocky couches; while their hard pillows would have made Jacob's blush for its fame.

Promptly at a few minutes after six the profound, terrifying African night descended on the land, and the unfamiliar stars came out. Through this blackness we trundled at eight on a rumbling trolley to a real dinner party.

Kavirondo Group

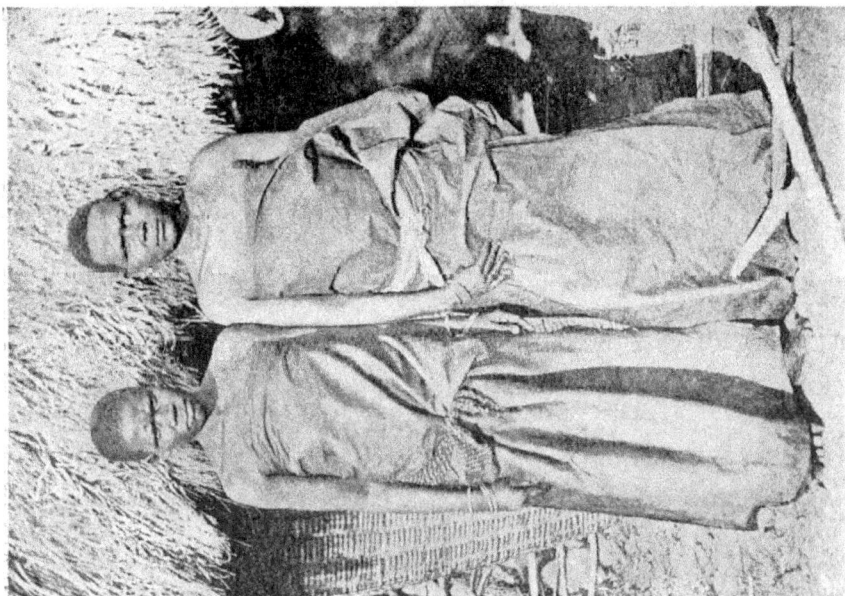

Uganda Women in Bark Cloth

FROM NAPLES TO MOMBASA

Wherever the English go they take the forms of life with them, so we found ourselves in a small gathering of well bred, well dressed people seated at a pretty table where flowers and shaded lights accompanied an excellent and most correctly ordered feast. Except for the barefooted, white-gowned and white-capped blacks, who glided noiselessly about, the occasion might have been at one of the centres of civilization. But the talk was of matters African; of the great loss in the recent death of the late commissioner, Sir Donald Stewart; of the murder of Mr. Galt by natives in Uganda; of the killing of another Englishman by an elephant, and the mangling of a third by a lion. By these tokens we knew we were in the Dark Continent. Also by a certain calm acceptance of fate. Those who have lived there some time get too used to the attacks of savage tribes and animals and strange African diseases to do more than comment in passing on the ill fortune of others. One must come to Africa to realize the blessing of the sense of personal security we enjoy in our occidental civilization.

CHAPTER III

THE UGANDA RAILROAD

THE savage racial struggles which have drenched Mombasa in blood date back to ancient times. As far away as Greek and Roman days the Phoenician mariners brought home reports of East Africa and its tropical wealth and its perils. Since which time, as related in a previous chapter, the Arabs and other western Asiatics have poured in, to be followed and fought by the Portuguese. In all of which sanguinary revels the native Africans have joined with fierce glee.

This continued till the nineteenth century, when — in fulfilment of the prophecy that the " meek shall inherit the earth " — the English firmly established their very excellent rule in the most desirable strip of East Africa, extending their influence inland and northward, so that it finally met their Egyptian operations in the Soudan, thus giving them entire control of the most famous river in the world — the Nile. This has not been accomplished without a tremendous outpouring of England's best material. Wherever you may penetrate, even to the uttermost confines of her sphere of influence, you will find men of high moral calibre, good education, antecedents and family, cheerfully accepting the most primitive conditions of life, and pay, that to an American would seem anything but exhilarating.

Mombasa — hasn't the very name a distinctively African flavor? — lying as it does on the low shores of the Indian Ocean, only a little south of the equator, gives the traveller a peculiarly vivid impression of the tropics in Africa. Colors, sounds, smells, all are intense and exciting. The tempered sunshine of northern latitudes is unknown here. Mangoes and other tropical trees cast dark splashes of shade in the fierce glare of the day.

Most of the dwellings of the Europeans are of the Indian bungalow style, low, spreading

roofs, airy, encircling verandas, and a general
effect of cool shade. The commissioner's residence, known as Government House, is, however, a unique and most effective bit of architecture. The lower part is of gleaming white
plaster, with a broad veranda whose snowy
pillars support the overhanging upper story,
which is of wood stained in very beautiful
and harmonious shades of green. It is situated
on a flowery point overlooking the Indian
Ocean, where it has the benefit of every wind
that blows. The death in October, 1905, of
the commissioner (or governor) of British East
Africa, Sir Donald Stewart, was a great blow
to every one in that part of the world, and
when we visited it a few weeks later the fine
residence already had an untenanted look, as
the turbaned Indian sentry paced softly up
and down, and the flowers blazed in the quiet
garden.

The older, narrower streets of Mombasa have
kept their mediæval, Portuguese look. Their
queer, irregular, closely built, white, stuccoed
houses do not seem to have felt the touch of the

twentieth century, except in an added decay; while the hordes of African and Indian races that swarm about in gaudy draperies are probably exactly like the hordes that for centuries have chattered and pattered in gay and odoriferous crowds in those highways and byways.

We landed October 17th, and, for those of us who did not get rooms facing the sea, whence came a soft breeze, that first night was a breathless, gasping stretch of wakefulness. The darkness was filled with strange sounds from the native village, whose peaked, grass-thatched huts, huddled closely together, covered a large tract in the rear of the hotel and of the main street of the town. At six A. M. the sun came up " like thunder; " the noises of the night consolidated into the low-pitched roar of the day; the hotel boys, white-robed, white-capped, barefooted and black, came to each door with the inevitable cup of tea or coffee with which every European in this country begins the day, and the hard beds and stony pillows yielded up their victims.

SOME AFRICAN HIGHWAYS

When, in the last of December, 1903, the railroad which connects Mombasa with Uganda and the great interior region was completed, there was opened to the travelling public one of the most curious and interesting railway journeys in the world. Before that it was a three months' tramp by caravan trip to this part of the Dark Continent; a way heavy with dangers and discomforts. Everything was brought up on the heads or shoulders of African porters. This overland trip annihilated all differences in intrinsic values, making a bottle of beer cost as much as a bottle of champagne. Bulk and weight were the only considerations in fixing prices. Now the railway makes the five hundred and eighty-four miles to Victoria Nyanza in forty-six hours, while a steamer completes the remaining one hundred and seventy-five miles in one or two days, according to the weather.

The railway is a metre-gauge road, the iron ties being imbedded in red clay, which latter sends up a fine, permeating dust. The road is none of the smoothest, nor are the car springs such as to minimize the rough jolting of the train. In fact, a favorite, though time-worn, jest out there is the assertion that the car wheels are square instead of round.

The railway carriages are like those in use in India. They are divided into two lengthwise compartments opening at the ends, and separated from each other by a couple of triangular, little lavatories, where there is an abundant supply of water to remove the red dust. There are three windows on each side of the compartment, and about a foot outside of these a boarding drops half-way down from the roof to protect one from the glare, the cinders and any but a very lateral rain. Inside there are shutters that can be raised a little over half-way up so that one can shut out the night or day and yet have plenty of air. The finish of the cars is of the plainest, and each traveller carries his own bedding. But two people in one of these simple carriages can travel with more comfort and privacy than in one of our over-decorated, over-upholstered, over-heated Pullman sleepers — always excepting our compartment cars. The engines burn wood, which saves one from the irritating coal dust that annoys travellers in other lands, but, as the cinders sometimes blow in through open doors and burn holes in the hand luggage, a watch has to be kept. Each person carries his own bedding and towels, also a good supply of food to help out in case of not arriving in time at one of the *dahk bungalows* where meals are served. The third-class carriages are built with the bare wooden seats set across the cars and are generally crowded with a chattering throng of Indians and Africans.

The building of this road was one of the heroic achievements of engineering, the men who undertook it and carried it through running every kind of danger. Many white men are said to have been killed by lions, while a still larger number of the native workmen met similar deaths. All along the way one still sees the arrow-proof structures, used for housing the workers, great windowless, corrugated iron shanties with protected roof-holes to let in light and let out smoke. Together with the dangers from visible and tangible wild animals and wilder tribes stalked the invisible and intangible danger from fever, which is still the constant menace in tropical Africa.

The sun blazed down ferociously on the railway station at Mombasa at the hour of our departure, 10.30 A. M. There was a seemingly inextricable confusion attendant on the setting out of this weekly train. Native porters rushed aimlessly about, shrieking, and reeking with perspiration. English officials, in pith helmets and khaki suits, shouted orders which no one seemed to carry out. The corrugated iron buildings and cement platforms radiated heat, so that it rose in vibrating waves, beating against our faces as we leaned out of the little car windows to watch the confusion and say last words to those of our steamer companions who were staying behind. At last, with a long, shrill toot, the engine started and we pulled out of the clamor and the crowd. We trundled slowly across the island, the whistle constantly screeching to shoo off the tracks the idly lounging natives who seemed to regard the rails as their boulevard. We steamed across the causeway connecting the island with the mainland, and after travelling some distance through thick groves of alternating palms and bananas we began to rise to the plateau, which at this part of East Africa comes near the coast. The dense foliage and plantations dropped below us, and gradually the beautiful panorama of the sea and land spread out beneath us, delighting us at every turn in our ascent with stretches of shimmering blue waters, fierce white coral sands and intensely green plantations.

The air became fresher and sweeter as we ascended. In a few hours we entirely lost sight of the coast and devoted ourselves to the new and interesting country which lay on either side of the track. After passing through the dense tropical growth of the lower levels we reached a region of thorn-trees, whose cruel spikes must have made the way terrible to the road builders. Gradually mounting we came to the bare, rolling stretches of the Athi Plain. Here begins that wonderful spectacle besides which even the finest modern menagerie dwindles into a little

Kavirondo Warriors

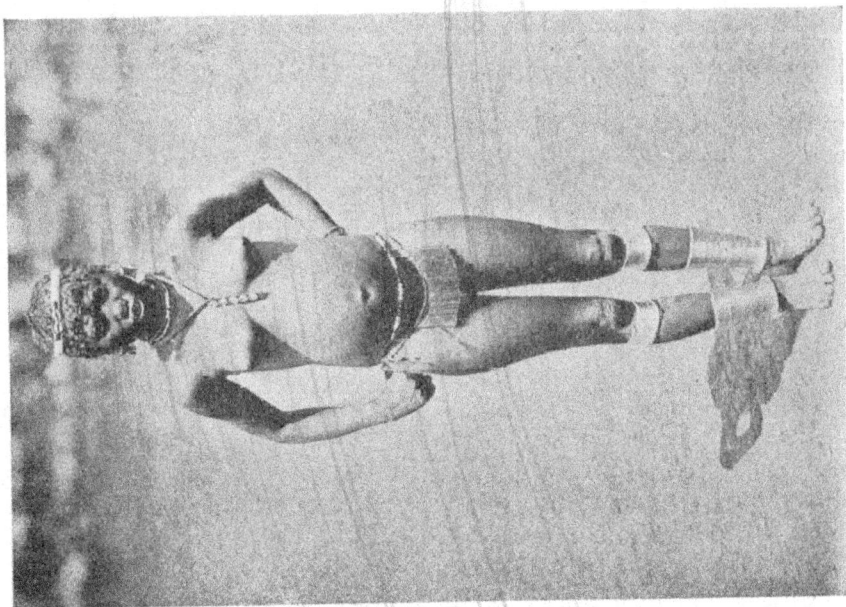

Kavirondo Beauty

side-show. This wilderness to-day looks as savage as when it was first adventured. The bare, reddish yellow earth, covered with sparse grass, rolls away to low hills as bare, which at sunrise and sunset glow with the most exquisite opalescent tints. At rare intervals a dry water-course bordered with scrub acacias would break the expanse. Or a patch of lean thorn-trees, whose level lines suggested Japanese art, would stretch away to the low hills which bordered the horizon. When we reached the Nandi and Mau plateaux, however, the land-scape changed, and green fields (some under a rude kind of native cultivation) and dense woods made a grateful change. The air too there was especially vigorous, clear and sweet.

What especially marked the way, however, was the extraordinary zoological show. Large tracts on both sides of the road have been preserved by the strict laws with which the Anglo-Saxon safeguards sport. The remote-ness, inaccessibility and lack of water in vast districts are, however, sufficient protection. The most hardy poacher would need a caravan to escort him. So, as they are practically unmolested, the strange African antelopes, birds and wild beasts pursue the even tenor of their way as if the snorting trains were not.

From the train we saw hundreds of zebras grazing near the tracks, while the grotesque Thomson gazelles — called Tommies — flicked their funny bushy tails as they capered away. The gnus, or wildebeests, big, black, and humpbacked, were also numerous, though the hartebeest was most in evidence. An awkward, ugly creature he is, with a shambling, high-shouldered gait and a head like an elk's. Of the gazelles, the Grant gazelle is the prettiest, with his black and white striped sides, golden back, graceful head and long pointed horns. Giraffes are frequently to be seen, though we did not chance to get a glimpse this time of any. But wild ostriches amused us by their awkward see-sawing gait as they ran from the train, balancing themselves by their wings. We saw some huge vultures, a few secretary birds, and many of the strange Kavirondo cranes, flashing black and white, with a dash of crimson. Our best bit of luck, however, was on the second day, when we had an excellent sight of a fine lioness, who, with her four cubs, loped away across a bare tract of land not a hundred feet from the train. Long, agile, dun-colored, she gazed at us over her shoulder with no surprise or resentment as she bounded slowly into the jungle, followed by her very plump offspring.

Strange tribes, as wild as the animals, gazed at us silently, or shouted at us in unknown tongues. Their faces and bodies were gashed with weird devices, the lobes of their ears being an especial source of artistic inspiration. Some of these lobes hung in long loops or festoons. In others incredibly huge disks of wood were set, or dozens of bead rings were hung, beginning at the top of the ear. Clothing was evidently much more a matter of individual taste than with us. Some were closely draped in gaudily printed cottons; others wore the scantiest of loin-cloths; while, when we came to the Kavirondos, a tribe living near Victoria Nyanza, we found a people of primeval simplicity, to whom a string of beads around waist or neck was clothing enough for men or women. It is curious to note that this is one of the most moral of the East African tribes.

Their high-peaked, grass huts were built in a stockaded circle in the middle of which we could see fires smouldering. The neatly planted fields about their settlements showed them to be a peacefully inclined people, though, like all the other tribes that we saw, their warriors carried spears and shields, or bows and arrows. They were tall, well formed, with amiable expressions as a rule. When these East African natives are cold they rub their bodies with castor oil and smear on this red clay, which gives them a look of garish savagery. Many from æsthetic motives treat their woolly heads in the same way, with quite a weird effect.

The temperature changed so entirely that the first night on the Athi Plateau we needed two blankets.

We were warned that after this night on the plains we should find ourselves and all our possessions covered with a fine, red dust to such a degree that our clothes at least would ever after have a lurid tinge. But by a rare good fortune the one rain, probably, of the year, fell then and we only found a pink cloud over ourselves where we had expected a crimson dye.

The largest interior town in East Africa is Nairobi, five thousand four hundred and fifty feet above sea-level, and a very popular place, though the meal we got there at the station restaurant was not as good as those at either Voi the day before or at Nakuru that same evening. They were all, however, much better than anything the traveller could get in the early days of frontier travel in our own country, well prepared by Indian cooks and well served by African boys under the direction of the Indians, who seem in this country the link between Europeans and natives.

Sitting at one of the two big round tables which accommodated the travellers at the Nairobi station, many East African celebrities were pointed out to me. One English peer was there who had just come in from the back country with his hair hanging to his shoulders in unkempt locks. Whether he wears it that way on Piccadilly I do not know, but it is a distinguishing characteristic of his out here. Opposite me sat a German who was one of the chief actors in the most famous lion story of East Africa, one which you will, if you go there, hear not once, but one hundred times. As it is not so well known in this part of the world, I will venture to relate it. This German and two Englishmen were among those engaged in the construction of the road and were to spend the night in one of the cars at Simba, a station at the eastern part of the Athi Plain (fateful name, for it is the native word for "lion"!). One of the Englishmen was to sit on the floor of the compartment on guard while his two comrades slept, one in the lower and the other, the German, in the upper berth. In the early, dark hours, those that precede dawn, the two sleepers were awakened by a horrid struggle on the floor. Neither apparently had presence of mind to strike a light. Perhaps time was lacking. In the snarling tussle the door of the compartment was closed and the two horror-stricken men crouching in their berths saw the outline of their midnight intruder against the faint outer glimmer as it leaped through the small opening in the upper part of the door, dragging over its shoulder the formless, crushed body of their companion. A few scattered, ragged remnants were all that was found next day of the man left on guard. He had undoubtedly fallen asleep at his post and been taken by surprise by a hungry, prowling lion. As a rule, it is only old lions who attack human beings. They grow too decrepit to be able to catch the more agile antelopes who are their lawful prey, so, goaded by a hunger which age cannot wither nor lessen, they pounce on unwary mortals. But this is the classic tale of East Africa, and the point made there is the marvel of the leap by the beast through the small window, dragging a man. I looked at the German with interest. In that country, however, every man has had his thrilling adventure, his narrow escape.

An example of a different kind of adventure

was told me by an Englishman who had had much experience among the natives. On one occasion, having incurred the enmity of some among the tribes with whom he was sojourning, he was much disturbed during the night by a horrible and suffocating stench. He could not investigate it in the dark, but at the break of day he did so, and found laid across the only opening of his grass hut the swollen corpse of a native who had died of smallpox. A pleasing bit of African humor, which, however, did not give him the disease.

But to return to the station at Nairobi. We did not stay there long enough to see the town, but from the station we caught glimpses of distant bungalows and of people riding and driving, for Nairobians are great authorities on horse-flesh and horse-racing and have their annual races. At Nairobi we shipped an armed guard to see us safely through the Nandi country, this energetic tribe being at that moment in revolt against the English.

This African tribe fights with spears and bows and arrows. The latter are usually tipped with a deadly poison of native brew, made from the gum of a tree which I was told was botanically known as *acocantherus shimperi*. No mention of this is made in Sir Henry Johnston's very exhaustive work, " The Uganda Protectorate," but as it is described with directions for antidotes in the official medical directions given to the English officers, its existence must be conceded. This poison is of a peculiarly deadly nature, causing almost instantaneous death. An Englishman who knows East Africa well described to me the effect on one of his own men who was struck by a Nandi arrow. When hit the native ran forward twenty or thirty feet, then spun around rapidly several times, and fell shuddering to the ground. The Englishman, his employer, ran up to him immediately, and found the man quite dead, while his body was drenched in a heavy, soaking sweat. In the printed instructions issued to the British officers who went into this war the surgeons advise an instant injection of strychnine, while the arrow, when possible, must not be cut out, but pushed through.

SOME AFRICAN HIGHWAYS

As we approached the edges of the great Rift Valley, the scenery grew positively familiar. We might have been travelling on the Lacka-wanna Road in Southern New York or Northern Pennsylvania, except that no roads nor villages broke the stretches of flowering fields, thick woods, or dotted the green hillsides. The many patches of thorn-trees looked like orchards of gnarled apple-trees. We had constantly the feeling that the next turn would bring us in sight of a town or a farm. Instead, however, we saw at rare intervals the straw huts of the natives, looking like congregations of haycocks. Sometimes these huts or kraals were isolated, but generally they were in circular groups, surrounded by a high stockade of elephant grass or of more formidable thorny brush of impene-trable nature. In the middle of these circular enclosures fires would be smouldering.

The afternoon of the second day we came to the eastern lip of the Rift Valley. Here dense forests pressed close to the tracks, forests said to be favorite haunts of wandering herds of elephants and of the formidable bison, the

Kikuyu Woman

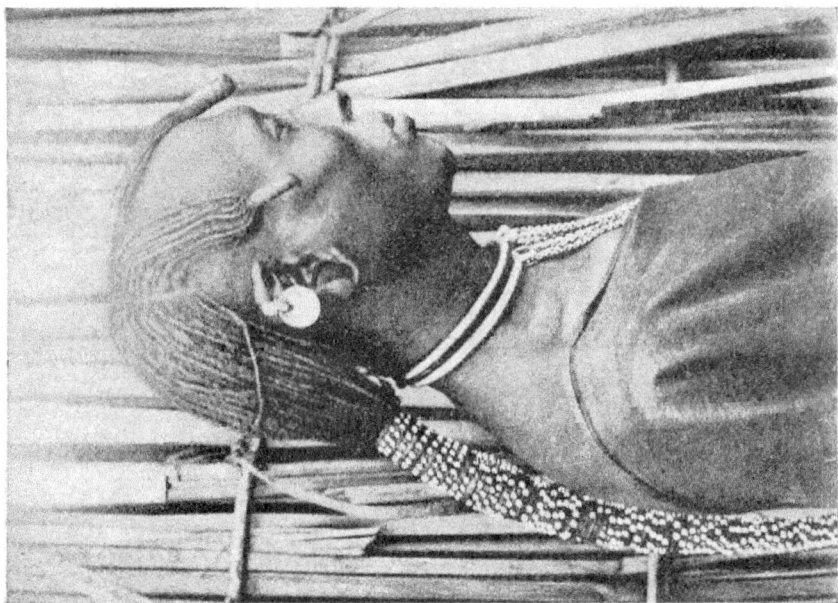

Wakikuyu

creature who always attacks every living thing as soon as his small, blood-shot eyes catch sight of it.

The divide which we crossed before coming to the Rift is eight thousand feet above the sea; and Mau, a resort, near its summit, is much recommended to sufferers from tuberculosis. The descent from the Mau Escarpment to the great Rift Valley was wonderful, both on account of scenery and from an engineering standpoint. The valley or gigantic gash runs north and south, and at this point is very wide. The afternoon sun filled it with a hazy glory, shining in and out of thin floating clouds. There was an impression of vast distances, and great, wild loneliness as we dropped with almost dizzy speed down nearly five thousand feet to the floor of the depression. Shimmering through the splendor of mist and sunshine, cone-shaped mountains of volcanic origin rose to the west, chief among which was Mount Londiani, while toward the south, like a phantom lake, Naivasha shone out of the pale pink and violet distances. Also Mount Longonot reared its pointed head beyond the glimmering lakes. It was dark by the time we crossed the Rift and were climbing the west lip to the Nandi Escarpment. Secure in our military escort, we slept the second night through.

There was a slight disappointment, mingled with relief, when our guard left us at six o'clock just at sunrise, and we had had no sensation beyond anticipation. Twenty or thirty Nandis had been sent to their long rest a few days before not far from that very station, which partly accounted for our safety. As we sat up, and our morning cups of tea were handed in through the windows, we saw our guard drawn up in line on the railway platform.

The black troops used against the Nandis and in all these little African wars were a smart-looking body of men, dressed in khaki with red fezes set jauntily on their heads. They are good fighters, obedient and devoted to their white officers, who are as fine and plucky a set of men as can be found in any service in any country.

It was about nine o'clock when our train

pulled into the station at Port Florence, but we had been up since sunrise, hanging out of the car windows watching the strange tribes through whose country we were travelling. We did indeed begin to feel that we were in the interior of a savage country, or rather of one inhabited by savages, for strange specimens of naked, black humanity swarmed along the road or clamored about the train when we stopped. It was all exciting and novel.

The first glimpse of Victoria Nyanza that one gets is of the long arm it stretches into the northeast and which is called Kavirondo Bay. After an hour or so dawdling at the Port Florence station, whose corrugated iron sides and roof and cement platform radiated heat, the train puffed out and trundled along to the boat-landing. The water looked as sparkling and eager as Lake Michigan on a May morning when we drew up on the little pier alongside the steamer that was to take us the last stage of our journey. Next to Lake Superior, Victoria Nyanza (Nyanza means lake) is the largest fresh-water lake in the world. But

Lake Superior has none of the hippopotami, the giant crocodiles, or the still more repulsive water-pythons that infest this body of water and give a sinister glint to the sparkles. By way of reassurance the captain of our steamer showed us photographs of huge crocodiles he had shot from the end of that very pier; also of a mammoth water-python which had crawled up a few months ago on the very deck where we were sitting, where it stretched its horrid, slimy seventeen feet of coils, and interrupted a " capital game of bridge."

Pythons, hippos, and crocodiles did not disturb us this trip, however, but left us to miseries more subtle and indescribable in the thirty hours' voyage to Entebbe, our destination.

Two very fine little steamers, the *Winifred* and the *Sybil*, which were brought out in sections from England, and put together on arriving at Port Florence, carry the main traffic on the lake. One makes the round of the lake (which takes about ten days). The other is devoted to the service of Uganda and the great interior region stretching westward to the Congo territory, and makes a weekly trip from Port Florence to Entebbe. Its arrival in the latter port is announced by a gun fired from Signal Hill, which causes each heart to thrill with the hope of letters from the outer world. You, who live in the middle of things, have no idea of the immense importance of news and mail to these remote outposts, where men and women of gentle birth and traditions live in exile — cheerful and voluntary, but exile nevertheless. The names of all passengers are telegraphed ahead, so that Entebbeans can know who is coming and make arrangements accordingly. The hotel accommodation is limited and very primitive, so the residents generally open their houses to the more noted visitors, and are renowned for their hospitality.

The two main steamers are most comfortably fitted with electric lights, neat little cabins and an excellent *cuisine;* and, as they are run by the government, are officered by the fine class of men England chooses for her colonial service, efficient, presentable, smart-looking men, who have seen life in every quarter of the globe. These two boats are supplemented by a small, historic craft, the *Sir William Mackinnon*, the first steamer on the lake. From personal experience I can testify to its ability to cause more exquisite human misery than any other vessel of fifty tons in the world. The *Sybil* had recently run on a rock and was lying up for repairs when we arrived at Port Florence. As the lake is uncharted the accident is not an unusual one. The imminent possibility of such a catastrophe adds not a little to the piquancy of travel on the lake. But the *Mackinnon* looked harmless that bright November morning. So, unmindful of the horrors that awaited us, we cheerfully embarked. There were an unusual number of passengers, eighteen of us first-class. The only cabin was small, containing but two bunks, and was already occupied by the largest cockroaches that ever clattered and rustled about floors and walls. So we seven women and eleven men preferred the small deck, situated astern over the screw — here we had our meals, and the tables being removed, chairs and mattresses were arranged for the night. These were laid as thickly as in an emergency hospital. With our heads in the gutter, or gunwales, of the ship, and our feet well mixed up in the middle of the deck, we spent what was for some of us eighteen of the wretchedest hours of life. At five in the morning some one said to me: " Can't you move out of the rain? " I feebly shook my head. An equatorial downpour was drenching head and shoulders. About three inches from my face the pink sole of an African foot was poised on the ship's railing, while its owner was letting down the pale green canvas to protect us somewhat. (Did you know that the soles of the feet of negroes, as well as the palms of their hands, were pink? I learned it then for the first time.)

On the other side of the deck a cheerful, but very seasick American, would sing out between paroxysms: " Home isn't a bit like this! " When morning came, for those who were not too indisposed, plates of unattractive-looking food were passed over our prostrate forms. To move for well or ill was out of the question, as we were packed in like sardines. Wind, rain and sun beat on us alike and found us torpid and inanimate.

The captain, a gay, good-looking chap who had spent the night on the bridge to avoid the sorry spectacle, came and inspected us with a wry face. As there are no lights on the lake travel by night is out of the question, so the steamers pull into some shelter and wait till dawn.

It was only when the settlement of Entebbe was well in sight that one melancholy passenger was able to rouse up, put on a hat and an all-hiding veil to face the welcome awaiting us. The long, low point of land to which the boat finally moored was filled with people, natives in fluttering draperies, and the English residents in conventional garb, the men in pith helmets. One dear, familiar face smiled out at us through tears, and the trials of the night's trip faded away like the mists of the morning. We had reached the haven, the first and most important halt on our journey. Our troubles were over. An enormously long train of natives bore our luggage off on their heads. We were placed in rickshaws and had a chance to look about us as we were pulled up the steep hillside to the main road of Entebbe — a broad, red highway beaten to a hard surface by the many bare feet that daily pass up and down it. The beautiful landscape of lake and shore and distant islands, with the brilliant gardens near at hand, made an indelible impression.

CHAPTER IV

ENTEBBE

A STRIP of red African earth, a garden gay with crimson hibiscus, yellow cassia, and roses of all colors, a broad stretch of sloping green fields dotted with strange trees of heavy, solid foliage, and then the lake, Victoria Nyanza, intensely blue, with a distant line of low-lying islands, the Sesse Archipelago, on the horizon, — this was what I saw when I looked out of my window the first morning after my arrival. Entebbe lies almost at the place where the equator crosses the northwest corner of Lake Victoria in the British Protectorate of Uganda, a little east of Central Africa.

In the foreground a swarthy native of the proportions of Sandow, clad lightly in a loin-cloth of coffee-sacking, was squatting on the ground and bending his mighty form and

General View of Entebbe, Looking Northeast

muscles to the cleansing of the kitchen dishes with the moist red earth. Other boys, barefooted, and clad in long white gowns (*kanzus*) and white caps, were flitting back and forth between the cook-house and the main residence. Of one thing Africa is lavish, and that is human labor; willing, cheerful, obedient, and not unskilful, the black man makes tropical Africa possible to the white man. It needs, to be sure, about four of these native servants to do what one white servant would do in any other country. But when you consider that they are taken from naked, free savagery and thrust into clothes, routine and order, their service becomes a thing to wonder at. *Dusturi* is their watchword. It means " custom," and, when once taught one way of doing anything, no power on earth can make them do it another way. If you would alter the arrangement of the furniture in your drawing-room, or the order of your service at table, you must get a new " boy " and inaugurate the change with him. To do otherwise would utterly disrupt and disorganize the one originally taught. But

in Entebbe there is no such " domestic problem " as haunts so many otherwise peaceful
homes in America. There is no awful presence
uttering the baleful words, " I tenk I go."
If a " boy " is insubordinate beyond home
correction he may be sent up to the administration and *pigared* (given so many lashes).
There are no " days out," no " evenings off,"
no " keeping company," and the housekeepers
wear an air of easy autocracy unknown in the
land of the free.

Entebbe (an English arrangement of the
native word *'Mtebe*, meaning seat or throne)
is a settlement of some seventy or eighty white
people and many times that number of natives,
situated on an elevated, wooded, and very
beautiful peninsula, projecting into the northwest corner of Lake Victoria. It is the English
capital of Uganda, which, as I have said before,
is an English protectorate. The native king,
a youth called Daudi Chwa, lives at Kampala,
the native captial, twenty-three miles away from
Entebbe. He is under the protection of England, who administers his country, levies,

collects, and disburses his taxes, and in short takes all the trouble of being a ruler off his shoulders, leaving him the glory. His father, King Mwanga, headed an insurrection in 1897 against the English, and, when that was suppressed, was exiled to the Seychelle Islands, where he died in 1905.

Until the Uganda Railway was opened up in 1903, life was very simple in Entebbe. The houses were wattle and daub, with native grass-thatched roofs. In the terrific thunderstorms which come during the rainy season — generally at night — the European dwellers in these bungalows often got up and dressed, so as to be ready to move swiftly out in case of the lightning striking and setting fire to their houses. Almost every one then living there had this experience at least once. Then came corrugated iron — that boon of new countries. This, well-connected with the earth, is an excellent protection, and to-day the low, one-story brick dwellings, with their overhanging red roofs, vine-covered verandas, and charming interior furnishings, make homes as comfortable and attractive as any to be found north or south of the equator. There is, however, enough to remind one that this is Africa. As there is no lime in this part of the world, a homely substitute is sometimes used: cow-dung, mixed with earth. This, whitewashed, presents a rough and not unpicturesque surface. The cement floors are generally carpeted with the pretty native mats or with fine Persian rugs from Mombasa or Zanzibar. Beds, too, are often of native manufacture. They are called *kitandas* and are made of strips of hairy hides, interlaced and lashed to low, rough-hewn structures. On these a mattress or two is laid, and, in spite of the equator, three blankets are needed, one under you and two over. (Entebbe lies some 3,700 feet above the sea, which fact does much to moderate the otherwise tropical temperature.) The illustration in the November, 1905, *Century* of the three-thousand-years-old bed found recently in an Egyptian tomb bears a striking resemblance to these African *kitandas*. To the archæologist this likeness might be more than a coincidence, suggesting as it does a chain of linking circumstance.

Each Entebbe house is set in a blooming garden, fenced in from the broad red roads by high hedges or fences made of *draecinas*, whose strong, green stalks are lashed together, making a most impervious barrier. The particular passion of the residents here is the cultivation of roses. Although they have other flowers, such tropical blossoms as crimson hibiscus, yellow cassia, and waxen, heavy-scented frangipani, it is chiefly in roses of all varieties, sizes and colors that their gardens abound. They climb over the houses, they riot in the well-ordered beds, and large jars of the cut blossoms are to be found in every home. That splendid vine, the bougainvillea, likewise grows here to great beauty.

Entebbe gardens also supply Entebbe tables with vegetables — some familiar, others strange, coming from India and the East.

The scourge of gardens and of houses too, however, in this country is the white ant. This curious, slimy creature breeds by the million, and burrows through bricks and plaster, eating everything that stands near the walls of a room, or within reach in the garden, destroying in a night the carefully nurtured growth of months. The queen ant is a most loathsome object, a round, fat white worm some four inches long, with a head like an ordinary ant's. Find and do away with her and that particular ant-heap is rendered helpless. When they burrow into rooms the ants bring with them a red earth deposit; in this deposit they sometimes plant a tiny mushroom, and it is not an unusual experience for an East-African householder on waking up in the morning to find a nice little bed of mushrooms in the corner of his room, which he can gather and have made into an excellent stew for breakfast. The white ants themselves are a dainty, highly prized by the aborigines here, and it is a common sight to see a native in front of one of the ant-hills, which are sometimes eight feet high, picking out the creatures. It is in the mating season, when they grow long, transparent wings, that the ants are edible. The dusky *connoisseur* covers the ant-hill with mats, burrows into it, and then, as the liberated ants fly up, they hit the mats, are beaten down, caught by the wings and are devoured by the African *bon-viveur*. If the *gourmet* wishes to put on real style he gets a friend to beat a tom-tom to rouse the ants to come out in dense throngs, when he swiftly gathers them. To the uninitiated it is not an appetizing sight.

As my brother-in-law's bungalow, though delightfully comfortable, was limited in size, he had had built for my use a cottage, with two rooms and a bathroom, midway between his house and the kitchen, where Nannina, the Italian maid, and I were most comfortably installed. To give us complete privacy, our entrance court was entirely enclosed by a high fence of thickly plaited elephant grass. Besides two feathery acacias which shaded this court, a young pawpaw-tree grew in one corner with a fine ring of encircling fruit. I was very fond of this rather tasteless, but exceedingly wholesome fruit, and with a jealous eye watched each golden globe ripen. But I was always foiled, for the natives are as fond of it as I, and would come by night and pluck the paw-paws at the psychic moment.

The roof of my room was separated from the walls by a strip of netting, which admitted a current of air, and added greatly to my comfort. At eight o'clock a boy would bring in my tea and fruit. At half-past eight two more would roll in the big zinc tub and fetch large jugs of hot water. At a little after nine breakfast was announced, and so the day began.

In Rome do as the Romans do — eat what the Romans eat, but, desirous as I was to carry out this rule, I did not get a chance to taste such delicacies as white ants *aux naturelles*, or a favorite dish the natives make out of an infinitesimal insect which haunts Lake Victoria. Out on the sky-line, twenty miles or more away, lie the Sesse Islands, the abode of the tsetse fly, and now almost depopulated by the sleeping-sickness. Occasionally we used to see rising from their distant blue forests what looked like curling spirals of smoke. If the wind blew toward us it brought over these smoky columns, which were composed of an infinite number of infinitesimal flies, — *kungu* flies, they were called, — that swept down on us in suffocating clouds, darkening the skies, shutting out the daylight, sometimes coming so thickly as to hide objects a hundred feet away. Even with all doors and windows shut they sift into the house. These are considered a great delicacy by the Baganda, who cook them in a sort of pancake.

There are many native Indian and Arab words in common use among the English residents in East Africa. As there are no telephones, written messages are sent from house to house by boys. These three-cornered notes are called *chits*. It is not the custom — *dusturi* — in Entebbe to have bells or knockers at the front doors; so instead of knocking the visitor calls out *hodi*, an Arab word meaning "hail." Also the servant who comes to your bedroom with a cup of tea calls *hodi*. I think that the custom arose with the Arabs from the fact that, living in tents, they had no door or lintel to knock, and it was necessary to call out. And the habit has become grafted on the life of their African neighbors. The Arab terms *Bwana* and *Bibi* are always prefixed to names and titles. In telling a boy to wait on my mother my sister would say: " Take this to the *Bibi* mamma." My brother-in-law was always " the *Bwana* judge." The maid Nannina was " the *Bibi* maid."

One learns quickly the few phrases necessary to express oneself to the native servants. The majority of these are Swahilis, from a tribe living near the coast. *Letti happa maji moto*, for instance, means " Bring here hot water." *Happana* means every kind of negative.

The garden boys — or " *shamba boys*," and water and wood boys, are, generally, Baganda (natives of Uganda). The best cooks are Goanese, a mixture of Indian and Portuguese coming from the west coast of India. These have a natural aptitude for cooking, and the variety of dishes which they send out of their primitive kitchens is wonderful. The stove is a sort of high brick counter, divided into recesses by more bricks. In each of these recesses a fire of twigs is built, and on these fires all the baking, broiling, frying, roasting, and stewing is done. The Goanese cook always sends in just enough of every dish for those to be served, but if an unexpected half a dozen or even dozen guests come in to dinner he performs the miracle of the loaves and fishes, for he never fails to produce a complete dinner, in courses, with enough of each course for the assembled multitude. This he does with hardly any delay and with never a murmur. In fact, he rather likes the extra tax on his resources. Each cook has always one or two *'mtotos*, or assistants, These are generally native boys, and as the kitchen is apt to be warm their attire is very light, and to peep into the kitchen just as a meal is to be served leaves a strange picture on the memory. The Goanese cook has the regular features of the Indian, his inky hair is long and straight, but his skin is almost as black as the African. He is dressed in white. His *'mtotos'* dark bodies shine in the lurid light of the blazing fires. The walls of the kitchen are black as the night outside, for, having no chimney, the smoke wanders about a good deal before it escapes through the hole in the roof, but never gets into the food. This latter is cooking in all sorts of strange utensils and sends out good and promising odors. The scene at night when dinner is preparing recalls some of Orcagna's wonderful frescoes of the Inferno in the Campo Santo at Pisa.

The servants' wages vary according to the experience and skill of each. The cook, or 'mpishi, get from fifty to eighty rupees a month. The head boy may receive sixty rupees, and from this the pay scales down to the water-boys, who get five or six rupees a month.[1] The servants all look out for their own food; the master is not supposed to provide any, though probably the scanty bits left from the table are eaten by the chief boys. In dealing with all African native servants, and this includes those from Cairo to the Cape, the attitude must be unremittingly that of master and servant. Justice and severity must be evenly mixed. A certain

[1] It takes about three rupees to make a dollar.

The Kabaka, Daudi Chwa (King), Uganda

Lumbwa Girls

distant kindliness may be practised, but none of the more familiar friendliness with which in this country we recognize the brotherhood of man even in the relation of house-servant and householder. Any leniency or excessive kindness is generally misunderstood by the native and results in an irremediable demoralization.

All the water used in Entebbe is brought in whilom paraffine cans from the lake nearly a mile away on the heads of the water-boys, who pass up and down the livelong day, supplying kitchen, house and garden. The fuel used is wood from the jungle, and such aromatic smoke comes from the hole in the roof of the cook-house, that one could fancy oneself within range of a swinging censer in a Catholic service. The lofty incense-trees, with their dense, pinnated foliage, are quite a feature in the landscape at Entebbe. The broad green fields which sweep down from the Front Road to the lake are dotted with them.

Where the ground dips into Victoria Nyanza, in sheltered inlets grows the beautiful papyrus in feathery profusion. Nesting in the shrubs which overhang a quiet corner of the lake, not a half-hour's walk from my sister's house, are hundreds of darting, twittering yellow weaver birds, their long, wonderful nests swinging in the breeze.

The Sesse Archipelago, which lies blue on the horizon, is composed of one very large island that is nearly divided in the middle, the two ends being connected by a narrow isthmus, and about eight or nine smaller islands, which, like the larger ones, are inhabited, though they have been devastated by the sleeping-sickness. Besides these there are countless islets and rocks.

The Basesse,[1] as the inhabitants are called, are great fishermen, and are adventurous navigators in their long, queerly shaped canoes. These canoes are a striking feature of Victoria Nyanza, their curious, disconnected prows rising and shooting away from the canoe like

[1] The prefix bu means one individual, while ba or wa means many. For instance, Buganda is one resident of Uganda, while Baganda is the plural use of the word. Lu means the language; so Luganda is the speech of Uganda.

the head of a pterodactyl or some other prehistoric monster.

Victoria Nyanza is said to be second only to Lake Superior in area among fresh-water lakes. It is approximately 270 miles long by 225 miles broad, with an area of 27,000 square miles. It is a shallow body of water, 240 feet being the greatest depth sounded. Its shores are fringed with many islands, so arranged, especially at the north end of the lake, to form a well-protected channel, which makes it safe for such craft as are on the lake to go from port to port. The centre of the lake is subject to sudden, fierce and dangerous storms, with frequent waterspouts. It is said that no boat has ever crossed the middle of the lake from north to south or east to west. There is no knowing what new features might be discovered there.

Besides the well-known denizens of these deeps, such as water-pythons, crocodiles, and hippopotami, native legends are built upon the existence of a strange monster called by the Baganda *Lukwata*. From the description of those who say they have seen it, " it might be," says Sir Harry Johnston, " a small cetacean or a large form of manatee, or more probably, a gigantic fish." The only European who has caught a glimpse of it so far has been Sir Clement Hill, who in 1900 was nearly capsized in a small steam-launch by a monstrous creature, which seemed to have a large, square, fishlike head. In vain, however, did I scan the calm and smiling surface of the lake for a sight of the *Lukwata*.

On land, besides the biting *siafu* ants and tics and jiggers, we were rather on the lookout in walking through long grass for puff-adders, the most deadly of all snakes, and *mombas*, a close second to them. I never saw any of the former, however, and only one of the latter, and it was a dead one in the Botanical Gardens. The puff-adders are said to be rather sluggish, and do not bite unless actually stepped on.

But one soon loses any sense of danger in the well-ordered days which distinguish life in Entebbe. Their dignified, leisurely system varies little. From breakfast till noon the offi-

cials — for this is an official station with little
or no business or trade — work at their allotted
tasks, while the ladies either stay well indoors
(on account of the equatorial sun) or don pith
helmets to superintend work in their gardens,
or do commissions. At noon comes luncheon.
From two to four is given up to *siestas*, even
the " boys " taking their naps then. At tea
time, from four to five, is much visiting, both
men and women attending to this carefully.
The tennis-courts, beautifully situated on the
town's green front, are energetically patronized
from half past four till six, when the sun drops
down behind the hills, and, with the bugle-call
from the near-by guard-station, night comes
suddenly. From six, to time to dress for dinner
at eight or eight-thirty, " bridge " is the order
of the day, for both men and women. There
is much dining and other entertaining here,
and when gathered about a table laden with
silver, gay with flowers, and lighted by shaded
candles, with all the wines of Europe and the
delicacies of Africa set before one, it is hard
to realize that this is the centre of a savage

land where brutal darkness and cruel super-
stition have hardly yielded an iota to European invasion. Not the least pleasant part
of the evening is the ride home in the gharri,
through the cool, silent, fragrant night, with
one barefooted boy pulling in the shafts, while
two more push behind, and a fourth pads
noiselessly along carrying the lantern. Every
one who rides or walks abroad after nightfall has
a boy with a lantern, to light his way. These
lights bobbing up and down the broad roads look
like giant fireflies. Even when there is moonlight they use lanterns, as snakes are said to
crawl about these shining nights.

No one can come to an English colony without marvelling at the skill with which the English turn a wilderness into an orderly, habitable
place. Here they have introduced the hours
and customs of the West End of London into
the heart of Darkest Africa, giving, in a short
three years, form, comfort and dignity to life
with a completeness that eliminates even wonder, so natural and simple does it seem. Yet
what other nation could do it?

CHAPTER V

A HOLIDAY IN UGANDA

IT was the King of England's birthday, November 9, 1905, and, to the furthest corner of the British Empire, the day was observed by English officials with what pomp and ceremony their circumstances permitted. In Entebbe, a royal salute was fired at eight A. M. from Signal Hill. Those of us who were not yet up were shaken out of our beds to a realizing sense of the importance of the day. Pulling aside the curtain, I looked out on the usual morning scene: a foreground of bare red earth, well beaten down by the coming and going of many unshod feet; the garden gay with flowers; the sloping stretch of green fields where the cattle of Entebbe grazed peacefully, escorted by their inevitable flocks of white paddy-birds who feed on the tics that feed on the cattle (nobody feeds on the paddy-birds). Beyond, the lake lay glistening and blue, with the Sesse Archipelago on the horizon. Near my window a half a dozen of the daintiest little birds were pecking at the crumbs that accumulate about the dining-room door; smaller than sparrows, sleek and comely, some of gleaming crimson, others of shining green, they looked as if just escaped from some rare bird-house. The two Irish terriers, Tim and Muggles, were chasing the nimble lizards which flashed, green and brown, in and out of cracks. Through the garden ambled, in single file, the water-boys, clad in raggedest sacking and balancing easily on their shorn heads the ex-paraffine cans of water which they had dipped up from the lake, a mile away. As the lake is supplied — as far as is known — not from springs, but from the drainage of its wooded shores, the water is quite soft and pleasant for bathing, though it has to be boiled for drinking. Not far away Joheri, the cook's assistant, sat on his haunches giving — from the earth under his hand — what might be called a dry wash to some kitchen utensil: He is like a splendid bronze statue of the most robust Roman period, while his head bears a striking resemblance to busts of the Emperor Tiberius in his youth, the features and shape of the skull being singularly un-African. Through the open window comes the aromatic odor of smoke from the cook-house near by, where some precious wood is being used for the fires.

Already the road beyond the high hedge is growing noisy with the voices of passers-by, while, through its interstices come flashes of the bright colors the natives love to wear; for every one is hurrying to the review of the troops which the commissioner is to hold soon. The troops are made up of a few Sikhs from India and the King's African Rifles, native soldiers under English officers, and a fine, sturdy, efficient body of men they are in their khaki uniforms. In the early days of British rule in this country the predecessors of these native troops twice revolted, once in 1893, when in one or two cases they not only killed, but also ate, their officers; again in 1896, troops brought down from more northern territories mutinied because of what they claimed (and not without justice) was a broken contract. Both were bloody insurrections bravely suppressed by a handful of English. And now they say that King Edward has no more faithful fighters than these erstwhile savages.

The review showed excellent training and was interesting as all military parades are. It was followed by a morning levee at the Government House, where the commissioner or governor received, in their order of rank, all the officials of his administration, each in the regulation full dress of his department. For even civil officials in an English colony have a uniform for such an occasion. Then came those not on the civil or military lists, all the merchants and agents *et al.*, and then the most interesting of all, the African chiefs in their full regalia of feathers, beads and gay deckings. All we women saw of them was as they passed through the streets to and from the levee, as it was a purely official function and no ladies were present.

In the evening the commissioner and Mrs.

Hayes-Sadler gave a grand dinner, also strictly official in character, and followed this with a general ball, which included every white person within a day's journey.

Government House was a charming residence, built on slightly rising ground so that the back opened out on a level terrace, while the front verandas were approached by a broad, hospitable flight of steps, banked on both sides by a beautiful collection of ferns and flowering plants. The wide, screened-in veranda stretched the full length of this side of the house, a hundred and twenty-five or fifty feet from end to end. The big reception-room, into which one steps from this, was high-ceilinged and of generous proportions. Its vast white walls were hung with the finest lion and tiger skins I've ever seen, for Colonel Sadler is an ardent and skilful sportsman, and these were all trophies of his chase. The room was effectively furnished with a mingling of eastern and western furniture; while books, photographs, and a profusion of flowers always gave it a peculiarly habitable look.

SOME AFRICAN HIGHWAYS

The night of the ball it was a veritable bower of vines, roses, and tropical blossoms, and well lighted with lamps and candles. The long veranda was hung with flags and draperies and one-half of it was devoted to bridge-players, for whom eight or ten tables were placed in a row with cigars, cigarettes, and decanters near at hand.

Here, as in all out-of-the-way frontier settlements, the men far outnumber the women. There were that evening eighteen ladies, and between seventy and eighty men, so partners were never lacking, and the dancers among the ladies were kept whirling to the point of exhaustion. Remote though we were from civilization, the assemblage would have done credit to any place. The women were exceedingly well dressed, and most of the men bore the unmistakable stamp of the well-born Englishman, while their smart uniforms were a distinct improvement on the conventional black and white evening dress. The music was supplied by a pianola, while in the intervals, from an excellent gramophone in a shaded nook

Review of Sihks at Entebbe

on the veranda, floated strains of Melba's songs, Sarasate's violin and other musical gems.

Outside at the foot of the steps squatted the rickshaw-boys, a cheerful, chattering crowd who evidently enjoyed the music and the revelry.

The supper was a triumph of culinary art, both in its variety and excellence. Every sort of salad and cold meat dish one could think of was there, including a couple of sucking-pigs sent over by the missionaries of the Sesse Islands; while puddings and jellies and sweet dishes of all kinds shook and quivered and swiftly disappeared before the sedately hungry crowd. Delicious red and white wine cups and champagne and other beverages flowed freely, and it must have been close to dawn when the last guest wended his way homeward behind his twinkling lantern. Probably some of the revellers thought they were following twin lanterns.

As I looked out in a pause of the evening through the vines that draped one end of the veranda, across a fragrant rose garden, to the tall trees of the Botanical Gardens and saw the stars grow in splendor as the glare of the dancing-room faded out of my eyes, I said to myself: " Can this be the equator? Is this what was so short a time ago ' Darkest Africa? ' Is that Victoria Nyanza? " Near at hand a gently bred lot of people were dancing to the tune of " Hiawatha." Others were gambling mildly at bridge; still others were drinking the wines of France or Germany, and eating salmon from the Columbia River, caviar from Russia, fruits from India and any quantity of excellent edibles from Uganda!

As a rule, except perhaps for an early morning stroll among the roses in the garden, we didn't go out very much before four or four-thirty, but occasionally we would don our pith helmets, order out the gharri (as rickshaws are called. in Entebbe) and trundle down to the shops, where there are more things that one doesn't want than can be imagined; blue, white and green bulbous glass articles; coarse muslins and Canton flannels; bright printed calicoes, and every kind of utensils and tinned goods at enormous prices. A sleek, soft-voiced Indian or Goanese merchant comes forward to serve you. Sometimes you may find a piece of bark cloth or some pretty native mats or basketwork which are worth buying. The bark cloth is a curious, rather unpliable stuff made by beating out the inner bark of a local tree, the wild fig. This is stained a soft reddish brown, and generally painted in some queer design in black. The natives wear this, draping it gracefully about them in spite of its seeming stiffness, which must soon leave it on use.

After doing our commissions perhaps we would stop at the club — a great institution — where ladies are admitted till six o'clock. There is an excellent library in the club, from which members can take books, and which supplied us with our reading during our whole stay. The latest papers and magazines cover a big table in the centre of the room. The crowded hour here is from six to eight, when all the bridge-players gather for a rubber before dinner; and all the other men come for a chat and a glass of whiskey and soda. This habit is pushing the Entebbe dinner-hour from eight to half past. The Uganda kitchens are not in the fell clutches of the Irish or Scandivanian "help," who has to be free for her own social duties at half past eight. No such claims are made on the Goanese cook, who, after his work, retires to some haunt of his own. To be sure he not infrequently gets drunk. But as he is apt to cook better under this exhilaration he is not much interfered with. His intoxication is generally manifested by a tendency to hit the other boys with a saucepan or anything he finds handy. A helter-skelter rush from the kitchen-house, accompanied by suppressed yells and laughter, announces such crises. But the dinner always appears in due order, without outside interference.

On the west end of the forked peninsula on which Entebbe is situated, is a huge banana plantation, covering a couple of square miles or more of ground. Roads wind in and out in a perplexing maze, and the place is an interesting one to visit on an afternoon's ride. To get to it you cross a low, rather marshy tract, where the coarse grass of the tropics grows lush and strong. All through this ride care must be taken on account of the frequent holes, made close under the surface of seemingly solid road by ants or by water erosion. It is no uncommon thing to have your horse sink into one of these traps up to his knee. Therefore anything like a brisk canter is out of the question. But there is enough to interest you to make even a slow ride pleasant. Strange Kavirondo cranes trail low across the sky overhead, looking as if they had flown straight out of some Japanese screen, the gorgeous red ruffs and smart black and white plumage flashing gaily against the deep blue sky. Underfoot perhaps we cross a caravan of *siafu* ants, a long, thick, shiny black line coming from the grass across the road to disappear again in the grass. Most horrid they are to meet on a walk, because if you inadvertently step on their procession they swarm quickly over you, and their bite is ferocious and exquisitely painful. If a house comes in their line of march they sweep it clear of every form of insect life before they resume their progress to parts unknown. Their front nippers or mandibles are like steel, and their tempers are anything but pleasant, so 'ware the *siafu* ant when you meet him!

When we got to the banana plantation on the afternoon in which I explored it, we found ourselves in a silent wilderness of these dull, but useful trees. A slight mist, premonitory of rain, had come up. Moisture dripped from the big ragged leaves. No bird or other life was manifest. The stillness, monotony, and sense of remoteness weighed on one. The horses' hoofs padded soundlessly on the damp sand. The road — so narrow we had to go single file — turned and twisted aimlessly, and was crossed by other equally narrow and aim-less paths. Sometimes the trees grew so close over our way that their great, flabby leaves flapped with wet caresses our faces and shoul-ders. At rare intervals we came on little clear-ings, where one or more grass huts testified to some human habitation. Where the in-habitants were that gray afternoon I don't know, as all we saw of them was an occasional shadowy form slipping in and out among the trees on either side of our road, and quickly disappearing; for the plantation was a thick one and a person could soon vanish from sight in the maze of its low, uniform growth. Too high to see over; too low to see under; the trees seemed to enclose us with a sense of helpless apathy as the twilight crept up that gray Sunday afternoon, and I was glad to escape out into the gentle shower which beat upon us as we made our way home in the fast falling night.

As a matter of fact, had the day been one of the usual bright ones of the country the plantation would not have made on us that weird and *triste* impression. It would have seemed merely a very large growth of useful banana-trees, — one of the main supports of the natives — the principal fact which enables them to live with the maximum of comfort and the minimum of labor. One sees them continually carrying great bunches of this nourishing fruit, which grows so generally. One of the most vivid mental pictures which I shall carry away with me is that of a Buganda woman, small, supple, well-rounded of limb, wearing a drapery of the richest indigo blue fastened under her arms, leaving her shoulders bare (a beautiful bronze), and carrying on her head a symmetrical bunch of green bananas, the two lower ones coming down like two green horns clasping either side of her head. The red road, which was her background, was glowing in the afternoon sun. The sky was an intense blue overhead, and the whole scene — the figure and the background — made an instant unforgettable impression of intense color and life, such as is to be found only in the tropics.

The only thing which forces the natives to work is the hut tax levied by the English. With clothes and food " growing on bushes," as it were, and a predisposition to indolence, no other consideration would rouse them to exertion.

They use the banana in various forms. The green banana, pounded to a pulp and cooked, is their chief article of diet. They also eat it ripe. They make out of it a sweet beer, and also a heady spirit. It supplies them with soap, plates, dishes, napkins, with material for foot-bridges, and they even use the hollow stems for pipes in West Uganda. It was probably introduced into Africa in some prehistoric time, though a wild species is indigenous there.

Before leaving Entebbe I must mention the Botanical Gardens, one of the features of the place. They are situated on the shores of an inlet of the lake to the northeast of the town and are a monument to the English love of horticulture. It is an enchanting spot, with walks and roads winding in and out of a wilderness of rustling palms, gigantic tree-ferns, massive incense-trees, baobobs, banyans, and any number of other trees of the tropics. These gardens were started by Mr. Alexander Whyte. Besides growing specimens of all the trees, shrubs, and flowers indigenous to that country, those in charge of the gardens are continually trying experiments with plants of other lands and climes, to see what can be successfully transplanted and developed in Uganda. The gardens lie on a steep slope of land descending to the marshy edge of a lake inlet, a spot supposed to be rather thickly infested with crocodiles. Indeed there are so many of these unpleasing monsters about the shores that there can be no swimming, a gentle sport which would be most grateful in that climate. They are said to prefer dark meat to light — but even the fairest blond would not care to put the theory to a test.

CHAPTER VI

THE SLEEPING - SICKNESS

THE cloud which darkens tropical Africa from the west coast, across the vast, unknown Congo region, as far east as the eastern shores of Victoria Nyanza, is the dreaded " sleeping-sickness." [1]

This strange, inscrutable disease first appeared in West Africa about fifteen years ago. It is thought by some to have been brought from South America. By slow stages it crept across the Dark Continent, attacking tribe after tribe, though the natives of Uganda have paid its most shocking toll. Out of a population of about three hundred thousand in 1900, two hundred thousand died of sleeping-sickness between that date and 1906 in the Protectorate alone.

[1] Sometimes called beri-beri, never correctly. — ED.

It seldom attacks white people. In Uganda there were, in 1905, when I was there, only two authentic cases among European residents. Since then Doctor Tulloch, one of the physicians sent out to investigate the disease, has died of it. He was infected through a cut in his hand while dissecting a monkey which had the sleeping-sickness. It is probable that this greater immunity of Europeans is due to the fact that they wear clothes. It is now definitely proved that this disease is communicated in Central and East Africa entirely by a species of tsetse fly, the *glossina palpalis*. The greater exposure of the surface of the body of natives renders them more liable to be bitten by this insect.

The first appearance of sleeping-sickness in Uganda was in July, 1901, when Dr. A. Cook, at Kampala, noted eight cases of a mysterious disease. At the beginning of the following year he reported that over two hundred natives had died of the disease in Buvuma, one of the islands in Lake Victoria. Four months later came reports that twenty thousand people had

132

Bakedi — Uganda Protectorate

Bari Tribe — Gondokoro

(Taken by A. Lobo)

died in Busoga, a district on the north shore of the lake, and that the disease was spreading rapidly. Still in the same year the death-roll was increased by more than thirty thousand, mainly in Usoga and on the islands in the lake.

In 1902 the Royal Society sent out an investigating commission, composed of Doctors Low, Christy, and Castellani. They arrived at Entebbe in July. To Doctor Castellani belongs the especial credit for being the first to discover the germ of the disease, the *trypanosome* in the blood. But whence the disease came, how it was conveyed, or how to cure it, were still unknown.

Colonel Bruce and Doctor Grieg came in 1903 to carry the investigations still further. In April of that year Colonel Bruce announced that the disease was due to a *trypanosome* conveyed by a species of tsetse fly, the *glossina palpalis*. This was a step farther, but the main problems — how to prevent and how to cure — were still unsolved. Meanwhile, death's horrid harvest continued, and by the end of that year the official records reported that in

Uganda alone over ninety thousand had fallen victims to sleeping-sickness. Whole districts were depopulated and laid waste.

In 1904 Lieutenants Gray and Tulloch of the Royal Army Medical Corps arrived in Entebbe to continue the bacteriological investigations, which two years later cost the latter his life. Having thoroughly established the tsetse fly as the sole agent in the spreading of the disease, it was found that this dread insect flourished only in damp, shady places — that it could not live far from water, or exposed to sunlight. In a tropical country like Central Africa it was impossible to cut down all trees near rivers and lakes. But about such important settlements as Entebbe, Kampala, and Jinja great tracts were cleared, while natives were warned to avoid as much as they could dangerous districts. Sleeping-sickness patients were, as far as possible, segregated and guarded so that the flies could not bite them, as, to carry the disease, the flies have to bite a victim of the malady. The germ then develops in the fly to a certain stage, when the fly can transmit it by biting a healthy person. The native word for tsetse fly is *kivu*, and in a pamphlet published in 1906 by Dr. A. D. P. Hodges, acting senior medical officer in Uganda, he says that the *kivu* has always been in Uganda, but its bite was harmless until the sleeping-sickness appeared. This pamphlet, which was also published in Luganda, the language of Uganda, was widely distributed among the natives and did much to help them understand the epidemic, its causes, and the precautions necessary to prevent its utterly devastating the land. The *kivu* never travels far from where it is hatched, but as a person may have sleeping-sickness two years and more before its most serious symptoms appear, and as the native Africans are given to roaming over great distances, the spread of the disease before it was understood was inevitable. But that the precautions advocated and preached by the English authorities in Central and East Africa were effective is proven by the fact that whereas in 1903 thirty thousand four hundred and forty-one died of it, in 1905 the mortality had been reduced to eight thousand and three.

By 1904 sleeping-sickness had spread to the shores of Lake Albert and the Upper Nile regions and was threatening the Soudan. Professor Minchin was sent out in 1905 as a zoologist to make a special study of the tsetse fly.

The fly is larger than our house-fly, but smaller than the horse-fly. Shaped almost like the former, its distinguishing feature, one by which it can be identified without fail, is that its wings cross each other when it is not flying. Its instinct is to bite; this it does ferociously and swiftly. But its bite is not dangerous unless in a district where there is sleeping-sickness. One lit on the neck of my horse as I was riding through a rather dense piece of forest one day; it was the only one I saw except at the laboratory. As I wore a veil and gloves, I was never afraid. Although close search has been made, the larva or grub from which the fly probably comes has not yet been discovered; its family life is still a mystery.

In 1906 the much heralded German scientist,

Doctor Koch, came. He studied the disease for a year, and then announced that *atoxyl*, a preparation of arsenic, was a cure. This was received with great rejoicing. But, alas, it has failed in the further and final tests. It may yet prove effective if used in the earliest stages of the malady.

The White Fathers, whose good work among the natives in Africa has long been famous, established in 1902 a hospital for sleeping-sickness sufferers in Kisubi, near Entebbe, but every one of their patients died, and they could do nothing to stay the disease, though they undoubtedly did much to alleviate suffering by their sympathetic and devoted nursing.

The best description of the disease itself, its symptoms and course, is that published in the Royal Society Reports of the Sleeping Sickness Commission. It is from Low and Castellani's report in 1903, and is entitled, "Symptoms and Clinical Features of Sleeping Sickness:"

"The symptoms of the disease begin very insidiously, some slight change in the former mental attitude of the patient being the first thing noticed by the relatives of the patient. Next, a disinclination to work, with a tendency to sit about and rest more than usual, appears, and at this time headaches and other transient pains may be complained of, especially pains in the upper part of the chest. The facial aspect now also changes, and a previously happy and intelligent looking negro becomes, instead, dull, heavy and apathetic. Once these changes have appeared, the disease may run an acute or more or less chronic course, progressing however to its ultimate fatal termination. It is about that time that one usually sees the case, and an ordinary inspection will reveal many of the following points: There is the dull, heavy, stupid look, a slowness in answering questions, and when speech does come, it is often mumbling, slow and thick; the gait is best expressed by the term shuffling. Headache, vague pains and chest pains may be complained of. The tongue may or may not at this time show the characteristic fine tremor, and in some cases this may also be noticeable in the hands. The skin is often soft, and smooth, or it may be slightly roughened. Glandular enlargements, common amongst all natives, may be prominent, but in some cases this may be very slight. The temperature — a very important point — is elevated, rising in the evenings to 101° or 102° F., falling to subnormal in the morning, the range often extending over four degrees or more, and the pulse of very low tension is accelerated, varying from 90 to 130 beats per minute. These two symptoms are of the greatest diagnostic importance in the early recognition of the disease. On interrupting the examination and quietly watching the patient, he will probably sit down, his head may nod, his eyes close, and he remains in this drowsy lethargic condition until asked again some questions. If one takes such a case into hospital, for the first few days a slight improvement may take place; the patient gets up from his bed daily, sits about the doors of the hospital, sometimes walks about outside, and takes a little more interest in life, especially at meal-times. Soon, however, depending on whether the disease is to run an acute or chronic course, the individual gets worse, he stays in bed more, becomes more drowsy and lethargic, though not actually sleeping; walking at the same time becomes more difficult, and he eventually remains constantly in bed.

" Tremors now usually become marked, these being of a fine nature. They are best seen in the tongue and arms. The skin may become rough and lose its lustre, but eruptions, though they have been described, are not common. Emaciation and general weakness become pronounced; the knee reflexes, which were at first somewhat exaggerated, become diminished, . . . and saliva often dribbles from the mouth. Drowsiness, which has gradually been increasing, now passes on to coma, from which the patients can only be roused with difficulty; the temperature falls to subnormal, in rare cases convulsive fits appear, and the patient dies in a complete state of coma. This is the common course of an ordinary acute case of the disease, the different changes taking about a month or six weeks for completion.

THE SLEEPING - SICKNESS

In the chronic cases the symptoms develop more slowly, and they remain more constant for considerable periods of time without any advance, but ultimately the patients pass into the late stages described above, and eventually die."

The devastation that has been wrought in this once well-populated land has to be seen to be appreciated. The harbor at Jinja at the north end of the lake, at the point where the Nile takes its first start for the north, a few years ago was filled with native craft of all kinds, dhows, dugouts, and the strange, high-beaked native canoes. Now there is hardly anything there but the weekly English steamer, and a few sailboats belonging to English residents.

Ten years ago one could travel through that country and subsist on food supplied by the natives — flour, fruit, vegetables, eggs and milk. Now each travelling caravan has to carry its own supplies as it moves through the ravaged region. On every hand can be seen deserted villages, empty straw huts, overgrown

gardens or shambas, whose whilom inhabitants have all succumbed to the dread sickness.

I went to the government laboratory at
Entebbe, which is the English headquarters
for the study of the disease. It is run in connection with a hospital for treating the native
sufferers. The investigations are carried on
by experimenting on monkeys.

The laboratory itself is a large airy room,
overlooking the town, the green shores, and
the beautiful lake, with the Sesse Archipelago
— the haunt of the tsetse fly — lying blue on
the horizon twenty miles away.

At the back of the laboratory, on the upward
slope of the hill, set on posts, are the boxes
for the monkeys, some fifty of which were peering at us around the corners of their homes or
through the chinks. Some few brave ones
sat on the tops and openly inspected us. It
was a curious sensation to feel that fifty pairs
of reproachful, haunting eyes were furtively,
but intently, fixed on us. Only one, a dog-
faced baboon, was indifferent to us. He sat

moodily gazing at the ground, meditating on his wrongs.

The monkeys, being caught in a wild state, pine so in captivity and are so sensitive to the altered conditions that they never live long enough to die of the sleeping-sickness. They are inoculated by means of the tsetse flies, but, much to the chagrin of the investigators, always perish from some other ailment.

Inside the laboratory are many curious cases, boxes, bottles and jars, and a queer odor of drugs and disinfectants, while in little netting cages the tsetse flies buzz and whir. A fly was dissected and analyzed under the microscope for me. Curious monsters they appear when magnified thirty or forty times.

An infected monkey was brought in. A native attendant held its arms and legs while the doctor took some of the blood. This was placed under a strong lens, and there I saw the fatal *trypanozome* wriggling in the fluid. It is shaped like a lizard and is in constant motion.

A dark spot appears in its semi-transparent

body, and if you watch this long enough you will see the creature divide into two wrigglers at this point. These two wriggle along through their æonian moments and in time become by the same process four. And thus I saw one link in the disease which has sent two hundred thousand natives of Uganda to their last reckoning.

Perhaps it is nature's way of keeping the balance, now that civilized nations have taken control of the territory and have practically done away with the intertribal wars and the periodic famines that used to devastate the people.

While there is nothing acutely distressing about this manner of dying, nothing to equal the terrors of other fatal diseases like cancer or tuberculosis, there is something peculiarly sinister in this slow, stealthy, irresistible approach of death, whose course no known remedy can stay or alter.[1]

[1] The following extract from Lady Lugard's " Tropical Dependencies " points to an antiquity for sleeping-sickness which I have not seen mentioned elsewhere in the accounts of the disease.

" Ibn Butata who, like Ibn Khaldun, was born in the North

Native Hair-dressing in East Africa

Uganda Women and Children

THE SLEEPING - SICKNESS

But the tsetse fly is only one of the entomological vehicles for carrying and communicating
diseases in tropical Africa. The mosquito is
recognized in all countries as an industrious
distributor of fever germs, and nowhere is it

of Africa, of Arab parents, though about thirty years earlier
(1303), distinguished himself by spending twenty-five years in
travel which extended over the greater part of the known world.
. . . The Empire of Melle, known to the Arabs as ' The Mellistine,
which rose in the thirteenth century on the ruins of Ghana, was the
first of the great black Mohammedan Kingdoms of the Western
Soudan to claim intercourse on equal terms with contemporary
civilization. . . . The curiosity which his (Ibn Butata's) travels
excited at the Court of Fez was, it is said, so great that the
Sultan himself wished to hear his adventures, and after listening
to him for several consecutive nights, ordered that the whole
should be drawn up and made into a book. This was done, and
the account, as it now exists, was finished on December 13, 1355.

" This may be regarded as the period at which Melle reached
its greatest prosperity. Mansa Suleiman reigned for twenty-
four years, but was succeeded by Mansa Djata, a vicious tyrant.
. . . He *died finally of Sleeping Sickness.* Ibn Khaldun de-
scribes the malady as being very common in his country, but
as this is the first instance which we have of it historically, the
symptoms as then recognized are perhaps worth noting. It
was specially apt, Ibn Khaldun says, to attack the upper classes
of the people. It began by periodic attacks, and finally brought
the patient to such a state that he could not remain awake for a
moment. It then declared itself permanently, and ended sooner
or later in death. The King Djata suffered for two years from
periodic attacks before he died in 1374. This practically ended
the Kingdom of Melle."

more dreaded or guarded against than in Africa. No experienced dweller there will sleep except under a mosquito-netting, no matter how hot the night, while the very careful take a dose of quinine once in nine or ten days, to prevent any latent microbe from developing. It is the theory there that to take quinine after the fever has asserted itself will turn the African malarial fever into that more serious disease known as blackwater fever. The African fevers have the most distressing way of fastening on their victims. After a long intermittent siege of them the sufferer may think himself immune, and then find that his immunity is only in Africa; that directly he leaves the Dark Continent he becomes subject to recurrent attacks of fever which quite disable him for life anywhere else — a most distressing discovery!

Some time ago a Belgian official appointed by his government to take charge of a part of the Belgian possessions in the eastern part of the Congo thought that his new post could be more easily reached by passing through

British East Africa and Uganda. So he and his wife arranged for their long caravan trip, which was necessary after leaving Lake Victoria, and had constructed a portable room made of wire netting. In this they proposed to live when not on the march. Besides the door there was a small opening through which their food was to be passed to them. The whole structure could be taken to pieces and carried by porters. In this way the Belgian travellers hoped to escape the fever. In spite of this, however, the man had a slight attack of fever, while his wife was dangerously ill with it.

But the mosquito is not the only carrier of fever. There is a disease called tic fever because it is given by tics; while the jigger gives still another kind of fever. The difference in these fevers is more in the microbe of each than in any outward manifestation of the diseases, and a person may have two or three different kinds of fever at the same time, which is very exhausting to the system, producing an anemic condition hard to combat.

Although as a visitor only the bright and

cheerful side of life was shown to me in Uganda, the other side was sufficiently evident. Disease in many forms menaces every resident there. No one entirely escapes fever. This is accepted with a plucky resignation which is the outgrowth of a certain fatalism which seems to be born and bred in life in tropics.

Besides this special curse of Africa, other spectres haunt the European residents. Smallpox walks the land. The natives have it so commonly that they often go about their work covered with its horrid manifestations. An officer in the Public Works Department told me that it was no uncommon thing to have a hand held out to him for pay covered with smallpox. I myself saw a tall, gaunt native stalking along the highway, in and out of the crowds, with the gray scabs of the disease all over his dusky skin. I was the only one who skipped to the other side to avoid him. While Europeans do not often catch this from the natives, there was a case of malignant or " black " smallpox in the house next to ours, the victim being a very good-looking, young

Englishwoman. She had, during a violent rain-storm, taken refuge in a native hut or kraal, and is supposed to have caught the disease there. There is only one resident physician in Entebbe to attend both Europeans and natives. He took care of the sick woman and of all other patients too. Two Gray Sisters were brought down from a Catholic sisterhood at Kampala to nurse her. Every day in their heavy, fluttering draperies they took their airing on the road in front of our house. There was no vaccine nearer than Marseilles. Never have I seen anything like the serene courage with which the residents of Entebbe accepted the situation — it almost amounted to indifference. Before it my mother and I were obliged to hide and stifle as best we might the panic which beset us. How many times at night I woke suffering from a fully developed case of smallpox! Every headache haunted me, until I learned that backache was the precursor of the disease.

If I ventured to speak of it I was always met with the tranquil rejoinder, " Oh, I don't think you or I will get it — and if we do — it is kismet."

Bubonic plague is chronic throughout East Africa, though it is confined to the native population.

Even given the best conditions, there is no denying that a long residence in tropical Africa has a disintegrating effect, both physically and mentally, on the white races. It saps the vigor, rendering bodies anemic and minds torpid. One of its most peculiar effects is the destruction of the memory.

"Oh, that terrible Africa!" said an Englishwoman to me on our way down the East Coast as we sat on deck one afternoon looking at the pink sands of Somaliland on the western horizon. "Already I am losing hold — I am forgetting — forgetting — things that I want to remember."

The mind grows cloudy. The sense of proportion is affected. Trifles assume undue importance. It is the wholesome custom in the English service to allow leave once in so often. Few stay in East or Central Africa more than two years at a stretch. At the end of this period a leave of from three to six months is granted. It is a wise generosity, as it is only in this way that the efficiency of their official force can be preserved.

The universal custom of whiskey drinking is much to be deprecated. It is not that it is ever taken to excess, but it is considered by many to be necessary to counteract the debilitating effect of the country by this stimulant. The climate creates thirst. Water is not considered as a beverage, therefore whiskey and soda is always forthcoming — very little at a time, but constantly. This is bound in the long run to tell on the system weakened by unaccustomed climatic conditions. Many a breakdown attributed to the tropics has been accelerated, if not largely caused, by this whiskey-drinking habit. Women do not, of course, share in it. Their drink is lime juice and soda, or claret and soda. They are, therefore, much less prone to the kidney and liver troubles that afflict the men in tropical Africa.

Nor are these drawbacks the only ones faced

by those who are carrying on the work of opening up that remote region.   No matter how hu-
manely, nor with how much consideration and
justice the natives are treated, that handful
of Europeans living among those thousands
of savages, offspring of fierce races, whose
chief joy for uncounted centuries has been
bloodshed, are in more or less constant peril.
Underneath the seemingly peaceful surface
lie stored up quantities of deep and abiding
racial animosities which might flare up at any
moment, started by an error of judgment
on the part of the English, or by a fancied
wrong.

On the water-front at Entebbe, at the foot
of the sloping green fields, stands a group of
warehouses encircled by a high wall.   There
now are stored the various supplies of the
military arm of the state, guarded by tall
Sihk sentries.   But the ulterior object of the
structure is as a place of refuge for the women
and children of Entebbe in case of an uprising.
Nearly a thousand miles inland from the sea, in a
tropical wilderness peopled by savage tribes,

the situation of that settlement, as well as of the many scattered stations in Uganda, is one of great isolation in case of any trouble or revolt. Their very sense of security is a menace to the European residents.

Nor are these pathological and warlike perils the only drawbacks to life in Uganda. The necessities of life, if attainable at all, are extremely costly; while all the luxuries, so dear especially to women, are only to be obtained with great difficulty.

The very throb which comes to each heart at the boom of the gun signalling the arrival of the steamer bringing news from the outer world is testimony to the sense of lonely isolation of the place. How eagerly are the newspapers, periodicals, and books exchanged! With what longing many a cultivated man and woman reads of the new music he or she may not hear; the new pictures, the new plays, all the doings and progress of the great world so far away!

The fact that the climate of the tropics makes it impossible for children to live there after they are three or four years old is one of the special disadvantages of family life. To bear children for others to rear is a heavy cross to many a woman in that part of the world.

To enumerate some of the lesser annoyances of life in Uganda, I must return for a moment to the tic and the jigger. Like sleeping-sickness, they both come from the Congo, and presumably originally were brought there from South America, where both are known. They are also creeping eastward with an easily measured tread, and the English authorities are taking what precautions they can to prevent them from getting to India, where they could work irreparable damage. Besides carrying a fever germ the jigger is in itself a most obnoxious and dangerous pest. Almost infinitesimal in size, it creeps in under toe and finger nails or into creases in the bottom of the feet, and, burrowing into the skin, lays its eggs in a little sac. These in time swell and hatch out and then the fun begins — festering, suppuration, blood-poisoning and all manner of mutilations ensue. It used to be a common thing to see natives minus toes or fingers as a result of the

Lake Ferry at Entebbe

The Sesse Islands

inroads of this insect. It is like sleeping-sickness, a plague of recent years, and when it first appeared was not recognized. Now it is well known, and the natives are so skilful in extracting the little sac before it has hatched out that serious infection is growing rarer. It is an interesting sight to see a native boy picking out a jigger's nest with a needle. From personal experience I can say that so skilful are these boys that they do it without causing any pain or shedding a drop of blood — though the hole left in the bottom of my foot looked as wide as a barn door and as deep as a well. Fragile as the sac was, it was extracted without breaking it. It was brown in color, soft, and the size of a small pea.

All insects in Central Africa are called doo-doos, and it is supposed to be advisable to wear white shoes and stockings when out walking, as the doo-doos are more visible on white and can be more easily circumvented.

In spite of the entomological perils of outings in Uganda, I shall never forget the charms of the walks and rides about Entebbe. Mounted on one of three horses the place boasts — a sturdy gray pony — I have taken many a ride through the dense tropical forests, where the horses have to go single file through undergrowth sometimes reaching to their shoulders. Strange trees grow in tangled masses, strangled by huge lianes or vines. Overhead an occasional troop of monkeys would go scampering and chattering along those wonderful highways of the Banderlog people. Every now and then we would catch a sight of the gray African parrot with crimson tail, fluttering in uncertain flight from shade to shade; or some more gorgeous bird, like the exquisitely tinted violet plaintain-eater, flashed across the line of vision. Suddenly would spring up in the path, as if from the earth itself, one of the silent, dark, lithe natives, draped perhaps in a strip of bark cloth or in some square of gaudy colors, probably, if it were a woman, carrying, at what seemed an impossible angle, on the head a round earthen-ware jar of water. If it was a man he would more likely be playing one of the almost soundless little native musical instruments, or carrying bows and arrows, or a spear. Overhead and underfoot was a lush growth of vegetation suggestive of centuries of damp heat; from the forest on either side came strange, stifling odors, as if the trees were sweating. Suddenly the woods would grow thinner; we would come to a grove of palms, through whose tall stems glowed the equatorial sunset, deep crimson, which we might not stop to admire, as the dark falls swiftly and we had to take the shortest way home to get there before black night overtook us. There is nothing as black as an African night, and I think that it is because the earth, being a deep red, offers no reflection to the faint starlight, such as we get in other lands. Instead it swallows up what slight glow there may be, and gives to the darkness a dense, velvety quality not to be found anywhere else. Overhead the stars glare more brilliantly than in northern latitudes, but they seem to cast no light, and the night is palpable, suffocating, appalling, and filled with a nameless horror which is quite indescribable.

CHAPTER VII

THE BAGANDA

ALTHOUGH our stay in Entebbe was too short to make anything like a thorough study of the country of which it was the eastern outlet, I soon grew familiar with the different African types to be met with in the throngs that daily filled the broad, red highway. I could readily distinguish the Nubians, who had come down from the north. They were, as a rule, much blacker than the Baganda, while their hair was curled into tight, close ringlets. Their general effect was of an inferior type. But the Baganda are superior to most African tribes. They are not so tall or fine in physique as the Kavirondo or Masai, but they are well formed and their features are much better, approaching the Egyptian type. In color they are a warm chocolate brown. The women are small of stature, and in youth deliciously plump and rounded in outline. They are a gentle, courteous people. Sir Harry Johnston, who travelled much among them and knew them well, calls them " the Japanese of Central Africa." They do not scarify, tattoo, nor mutilate their bodies in any way, and among the men have always been most scrupulous in regard to the decency of their attire, being particular to drape the bodies completely. They incline to a very classic style in the folds of their garments. For some reason, which I never could work out, the women are obliged to wear their draperies brought around under their arms, leaving shoulders and arms bare. Not many years ago there was a death penalty for any woman who brought hers over her shoulders. However, when the first white traveller visited Uganda, the female valets of King M'tesa went stark naked about the palace at Mengo.

The legend of the country is that its first resident was Kintu, a man who came from the north, bringing his wife and one cow, one goat, one sheep, one chicken, one banana, and one sweet potato. In less than a twelvemonth all of these, beginning with his wife, increased and multiplied, so that in a few years the country was settled entirely with the descendants of Kintu, living off the produce which sprang up from the live stock, chicken, banana, and sweet potato which he first introduced. Having so successfully started the nation, he and his prolific wife wandered away and disappeared. To this day there are natives who look for their return at some great national crisis.

Sir Harry Johnston gives a more probable, though less picturesque, account of the settlement of Uganda. He writes that a mighty hunter called Muganda (meaning " brother ") first came from the north and by his prowess collected followers and established a nation, giving his name to the country, which he called Uganda. The language is known as Luganda, the individual as Buganda, the tribe as Baganda, as before related.

The first visitor from the outer world to come into the Uganda was a Baluch soldier, named Isau bin Hussein, of Zanzibar, who, in 1849 or '50, flying from his creditors, finally reached the court of Suna, King of Uganda. On account of his beard they named him " Muzagaya " (" The Hairy One "), and he became a power in the land. Through him the people there first heard of the Arabs and of white men, of whose existence only vague reports — treated as fairy tales — had hitherto reached them. The rumor arose among them that they too were originally descended from a white race. Their legends recorded that in the days of their first occupation their skins were lighter and their hair longer. The rumor ended in a prophecy that from the northeast should come a white race who would conquer them. So when years later Bishop Hannington sent word from the country northeast of them to ask if he might enter their territory by that route, permission was refused him. When he persisted and pushed on and into Uganda he met his death, for they thought he was but the precursor of the dreaded invasion, which did indeed eventually come, thus fulfilling the prophecy.

The language is most melodious, especially

when spoken by the soft, rich voices of the Baganda. Their salutation is quite elaborate. I tried to learn it, but never could quite grasp the soft and often repeated vowels and grunts:

" Otiano! "

" Otia! "

" Otiano! "

" Aa! "

" M'm! "

and so on, with brilliant smiles, in this manner would the bolder natives greet me on the broad Kampala Road.

What a place this road was! The low mud houses, or more pretentious corrugated iron ones, faced each other on either side of an enormously broad highway, whose red earthen surface was hard beaten by much passing. The courts were held in a comfortable building at the main corner, where the Front Road meets the Kampala Road. It was a one-story structure, with verandas on the east front and windows on all four sides, open to the breeze. It was guarded by *askaris* or native police in khaki uniforms.

THE BAGANDA

A little beyond the fort was the hospital, a charming building, whose big, airy rooms were devoted to the use of such officials and their wives as were too ill to be properly cared for at their own homes. Behind the hospital, higher up on the hillside, was the native hospital, including the house where the sufferers from sleeping-sickness were treated. Next door to the lower main building was the government laboratory, described in the chapter on sleeping-sickness. On the opposite side of the road was the rest-house, a long, low building, where those who come in from *safari* (caravan trip) could " bed down," and get shelter.

The rainy seasons in Uganda are from September to November and from March to May. July is the driest month of the year. Then the roads dry up and pulverize into the fine, red dust, which permeates clothes and houses. We arrived a little late for the heaviest rains, though we got some downpours. But we had no samples of the terrific thunder-storms which are such a menace to that country, for which I am devoutly thankful. We could see fierce ones, however, pursuing each other around the wide horizon. It is the theory of Entebbeans that the extensive cutting down and thinning out of the forests on their peninsula has had an effect rendering that particular spot less liable to these electric storms. The descriptions of Sir Harry Johnston and other African travellers of these thunder-storms quite reconcile one to their omission.

The wide Front Road is bordered on one side by high hedges, through which one catches glimpses of lovely, flowering gardens and cosy looking bungalows. While on the other side the land slopes in broad green fields to the lake. Entebbe cattle, humped back and wide horned, graze on these meadows. Tall, thick-foliaged incense-trees grow each in solitary state in scattered clumps, while ant-hills of varying sizes and shapes further diversify their grassy sweep. Half-way down the Front Road are the tennis courts, where every afternoon the men and women of the station meet to play. Further down the hill the cricket-ground lies enclosed by a fence with a club-house to the west, where, from a wide veranda, lookers-on can watch the weekly match.

The Front Road is bordered by an orderly row of lime and orange trees. At its east end the tall trees which shade a beautiful residence and garden, planned and built by Colonel Coles, are full of chattering, scampering monkeys, among which my brother-in-law pointed out to me a colobus monkey, white-faced and plumy tailed. A peculiarity of this species of monkey is that it has no thumb, its place being marked, if at all, by a minute excrescence bearing a tiny nail. It is a species only known in Africa, and its name is the Greek for " mutilated."

The currency of Uganda is that of East Africa, the Indian currency of rupees and annas. But the natives still use the strings of cowry shells which have been their money from time immemorial. These cowry shells are brought from the coast of Zanzibar, and in pre-railroad days, when they were brought up by overland caravans, represented more of human labor than they do now. The Baganda wear them about their necks, and accept them in pay for work.

The basketwork of the Baganda is one of the specialties of the country. So finely can they weave that they can make bottles which will hold milk. They also make a sort of pottery, in most artistic shapes, ornamented by designs of a classic effect, and finished with a rich black glaze. This pottery is unfortunately so friable that it is almost impossible to transport it without breaking it. They also make pipes of this same pottery in most graceful forms.

Of the harp of Uganda, Sir Harry Johnston writes that it is " interesting because its identical form is repeated in the paintings of ancient Egypt, where the instrument must have had its origin."

Besides this harp they have lutes, and an instrument like a xylophone, and various kinds of tom-toms, the native drums which throb from one end of Africa to the other with savage rhythm, through forests and across plains.

The Baganda, lying in a remote and inac-

"Lender" Women (Nubian)

cessible region, were not so devastated as
other tribes by the slave-trade which flourished
so many centuries in East Africa. They have
welcomed the apparent advantages of civilization, and have shown a keener appreciation of
these advantages than other East African natives, but they have at the same time clung
closely to their original organization, maintaining their court and king at Mengo (or Kampala,
as the European quarter of the settlement
is called).

At this point it will not be out of place to
tell the story of the murder of Harry Galt,
which was absorbing attention while we were
in Entebbe, where the murderers were being
tried.

On May 19th, 1905, Harry St. George Galt,
who was acting sub-commissioner in a distant
district in Uganda, was murdered by a native
at Ibanda camp. The news, brought by runners,
was a great shock to the foreigners in Uganda
and East Africa.

Before going into the details of the incident
two factors must be considered — significant,

underlying, racial characteristics. The first is the passion some young Englishmen have for savage solitudes, far from the madding crowd. It is this intense love of utter personal freedom, and sense of personal power, combined with a real joy in danger, which qualifies so many of them to go alone to wild and inaccessible regions, among wild tribes, and there establish and maintain order. Men who have once tasted this life are apt forever afterwards to find civilization and its conventional restrictions irksome. To us the settlement of Entebbe seemed the very outpost of the world. To those officials who came from the interior, where they probably had not seen a white person for months, it seemed next door to London, and its strict observance of social customs soon drove these lovers of freedom back to their solitudes, rejoicing; while many of those officials whose duties kept them at Entebbe sighed for the liberty of remote stations.

We Americans are, as a rule, gregarious, lovers of cities, and frequenters of highways.

THE BAGANDA

The impulse which enables Great Britain to cope successfully with wildernesses is almost lacking in our make-up, and I never got over the wonder of the spectacle of these splendid types of British youth, gently born and bred, delighting in their lonely and often perilous strife with savage conditions.

And, to go on to the second racial trait; there is that in the wild peoples among whom the English live in Africa which is always eluding outsiders, a certain profound racial hatred and antipathy, that rarely shows on the surface, but which exists nevertheless, and manifests itself in such acts as the murder of Harry Galt. The natives of East Africa and of Uganda resent the British dominion. They cannot shake it off. They live in apparent amity, and they try to enjoy a civilization which is antipathetic to them. They hate work and they love fighting. The English force them to toil and have almost abolished their bloody intertribal wars. Apparent peace reigns, but the instincts and tendencies of savages can only be checked, not altered, in a couple of generations.

Harry St. George Galt was a fine specimen of Anglo-Saxon manhood; a plucky young fellow, a good shot, a good friend, what would be called " a good all around sport; " and had a widowed mother and sister dependent upon him. He was more than usually popular with the natives among whom he lived. Yet on the above date as he sat in front of his grass hut a young native, named Lutakara, came up and, without warning, stabbed him, running a spear into his lungs near his heart. Galt was alone at the time and according to the report of his own native servants ran to the cook's hut and, gasping out that he had been killed, fell to the ground, the blood gushing from his mouth and from the wound. He died in a few minutes, far from his kind, in an African forest with only African savages about him.

The murderer was in his turn killed almost immediately by two other natives, Gabrieli and Isaka, and therein lies the mystery of the affair, for evidence was brought out at the trial which proved that the slayers of Lutakara had themselves incited him to the deed. Their motive in doing away with him was to abolish his evidence and to establish themselves with the English as avengers of British wrongs.

Some years before Lutakara's brother had died, supposedly from an impure vaccination performed by an English doctor. The conspirators are thought to have so worked on the surviving brother's feelings as to have incited him to revenge by murder. Galt was the nearest white man. He was alone and accessible; so the deed was done. The motive of Gabrieli and Isaka and others working with them is, however, further to seek. With some the theory was that their inspiration came by indirect channels from the court of Uganda at Kampala, where the young king sits surrounded by his chiefs; nominally under the protection of England; practically under her direction and suzerainty. But this could not be proved. All the mystery of the Dark Continent shrouded the case beyond the proved complicity of Gabrieli, Isaka and some minor actors in the drama.

SOME AFRICAN HIGHWAYS

There are certain workings of the African mind which no white man can follow or fathom. A glint here and there shows a hidden world unknown. These childlike, black races have some savage potentialities, which give a sinister quality to their *naivete*. Friendly as they may appear to be, devoted as they certainly are in individual instances, it is a fact that the black races *do not like the white people.* The tenure of the Anglo-Saxon in Central Africa is rather like that of the animal trainer in a cage full of trained lions and tigers.

The trial of those connected with the murder of Mr. Galt was held in the High Court of Uganda, sitting in Entebbe during our stay there, and we were much interested in it. It was tried under Indian laws and court procedure, so there was no jury. The lawyers on both sides presented their cases. The judge summed up the evidence and pronounced sentence.

The court-house is a long, one-story building, with projecting roofs, and stands on a fine, overlooking site. At one end of the large, bare court-room the judge sat, in wig and gown, on a raised platform. The prisoners in wooden, open pens stood below him, to the left, guarded by native soldiers in khaki uniforms. To the right sat the lawyers, also in gowns. One of the prisoners, Isaka, had a fine head, almost classic in lines. The others were of the ordinary Waganda type, clean-limbed, not large, nor very black. The court-room was packed with a large percentage of natives among the onlookers. The windows on all four sides were open, and warm noonday breezes came through, while outside more natives could be seen lounging about, and beyond lay the green fields and woods sloping to the broad, glassy stretches of the lake.

The conduct of the case was exemplary. Each side was stated clearly and briefly. Witnesses were examined carefully, by means of an interpreter, due respect being given to even the most trivial evidence; and there was much that was childish, as all the witnesses were natives, and they wandered and became involved in their testimony. But out of it all a clear case was evolved on which the judge based his summing up and sentence. The latter was hanging for the two principals and imprisonment for varying terms for the other prisoners.

The serious dignity which characterized the trial, the conciseness with which each side presented its case, the lack of forensic display, together with the care for justice, made a deep impression on me. We Americans would have been more dramatic in arriving at similar ends.

As a parting gift my brother-in-law gave me the kiboko, or rhinoceros hide whip, which Mr. Galt always carried with him through African solitudes, swamps, and jungles, which was hanging on his wrist when he was murdered, and which now hangs in my room. I never knew Mr. Galt, but the sight of that rude leathern thong often brings up, not only the vision of that brave young Englishman, the only son of a widow, but of all the other plucky fellows who are out there in those wildernesses working out the destiny of the Dark Continent. The pay they get is small, the praise they get

THE BAGANDA

is hardly larger, but the joy that is theirs in the work, in the loneliness, and in the danger is exceeding, and worth all the rest put together.

CHAPTER VIII

LEAVING ENTEBBE

IT was with a real pang that I looked my last on the wooded hills and green fields of Entebbe. As the steamer, the *Sybil*, was starting early in the morning, we went on board the night before. The ride down in the gharries through the fragrant darkness, with swinging lanterns, was a quick one, as the way was mostly down hill, and the barefooted gharri-boys sped soundlessly between the shafts.

We had left a new member of the family up in the cosy home, in the pretty garden; a tiny morsel of humanity who had arrived ten days before, and who didn't think it at all strange that he should be born in the heart of the Dark Continent, just where the equator crosses Victoria Nyanza. The eager joy of the house-boys over his arrival was pretty to see.

184

Muhuma Cowman, Uganda Type

Natives Catching and Eating White Ants — Uganda

Into the room where he lay by his mother's side they crept silently one by one, long before we were admitted to see the pair, and bending over him murmured, in their soft, rich voices, " *M'suri* " (" beautiful ").

We steamed out of Entebbe harbor early next morning. The *Sybil* was a gleaming white, smart-looking, 250-ton steamer, which, with her twin sister, the *Winifred*, had been brought out in sections from England and put together on arriving at the lake. She was a most comfortable little vessel, with electric lights, nice cabins, the first porcelain tub we had seen in Africa and an excellent *cuisine*. The *Winifred* was making the round of Victoria Nyanza, there being a contract with the German government to provide a regular service for the German ports at the southern end of the lake.

The day was an exquisite one, and the trip along the coast gave us a series of charming views. The shores rose abruptly from the water and were clothed in forests alternating with open stretches of green grass. To the east and south an almost unbroken chain of islands dotted the lake. There was no sign of human habitation, though with the aid of field-glasses I saw one settlement of the pointed roofs of native kraals, looking like haycocks. I was told that whereas it had once been a thriving village, only two women lived there now, all the other inhabitants having died of sleeping-sickness. I suppose these two did not join any other community owing to a characteristic peculiar to African natives, that is, an ineradicable unfriendliness between tribes. Within the limits of a tribe or community they will share with each other and give mutual aid; but there are no intertribal relations. Six years before at Tanga I had seen natives dying and dead in the streets — perishing from famine, while their fellow Africans looked on with indifference and gave them no aid, because the sufferers were from the interior.

The waters of the lake rippled in the morning sun. The steamer ploughed merrily along. How different from our trip of five weeks before! The second officer, the same good-looking youth who had convoyed us in the

LEAVING ENTEBBE

Sir William Mackinnon, was engaged in painting the benches on the immaculate deck where we sat. To one railing clung a monkey, jabbering and eating bananas. On another a gray parrot squawked harshly. I turned to and helped paint the seats with great effect. The other passengers — of whom there were a half a dozen — lounged about in long steamer-chairs. One of the loungers was Mr. Freshfield, the celebrated mountain climber, who had come out to Uganda to attempt the ascent of Ruwenzori. He had not only failed, but had returned to Entebbe with three kinds of fever microbes rioting in his system, and had had just strength enough to crawl from the hospital to the steamer, a very ill man. Since then two Europeans have made this ascent; one whose name I've forgotten, while the second was the Duke of Abruzzi (cousin to the King of Italy), who was much disgusted that he was not the first.

I remember that at luncheon that day on the *Sybil*, we had a delicious curry made by the Indian cook. It takes an Indian to make a *pukka* curry, and when well made it is *the* dish for the tropics.

About three o'clock that afternoon we steamed into the pretty, almost enclosed harbor of Jinga. Here we laid up for the night. Before the days of the sleeping-sickness this bay was well filled with native crafts of all kinds, dugouts and dhows. Now but few were to be seen. We had here our first ride in a real dugout, for when a kind resident of Jinja came to show us the sights of the place he took us ashore in one of these curious and utterly African boats. It was between thirty and forty feet long, hollowed out of the trunk of a tree, and paddled by about twenty sturdy natives, with round flat paddles, like big wooden soup-spoons. As we rounded the end of the pier it looked as if a collision was imminent between our unwieldy craft and a huge lighter swinging slowly and heavily about, which would mean a pleasant feast for lurking crocodiles. But with much yelling and paddling our boys gave our dugout a lurching twist and landed us at the steps.

190

LEAVING ENTEBBE

The principal sight of Jinja is the Falls of Ripon, the place where the waters of this great lake slip over the rocks and start on their way via Uganda, the Albert Nyanza, the Soudan, and Egypt to the Mediterranean. To see this, the most famous and historic of the world's great rivers, at its inception, is a distinct sensation. Hitherto we had only felt the utter remoteness of this corner of the world, its isolation and savage loneliness. But these waters that flowed slowly under the keel of our boat were going around that point of land to tumble into that flood which would eventually roll by Khartoum, and on by those famous ruins, those splendid tombs, those historic places, to Cairo and the Mediterranean.

On landing at Jinja one is first struck with the vast tract of utterly bare, red earth which fronts the settlement, sloping thence to the lake. This has been denuded of all vegetation in the hopes of thus driving away the fever-bringing mosquito which especially haunts these shores of the lake. To the right as you walk up the bank lies the military camp — a neat-looking enclosure. Further on and almost out of sight is the native town where the Indians and Africans live in corrugated iron shanties and grass huts. Here are also the stores of the traders. To the left, near the bare summit of the low hill, are the inevitable tennis-courts which the English dweller in the tropics sets up as soon as he does his house, to give him the exercise so difficult to achieve otherwise in this climate. Further on are the three or four dwellings of the Europeans, for Jinja, though an important post, is a small one, the only white woman living there being the wife of the sub-commissioner. Coming from well-wooded and flower-embowered Entebbe, this place, without trees or foliage of any kind, looked bare and unattractive. Yet each house stood in its little enclosure, where some attempt at cultivating flowers and vegetables was made.

Leaving the settlement we struck off to the west through a region of high grass and low shrubs in the heat of a very fervid afternoon sun to see the falls. Where the narrow path necessitated single file, my guide went ahead on account of possible danger from the leopards which are plentiful in this neighborhood; also to scare away any momba, or puff-adder, or other poisonous snake that might be in the way. On the soft red earth of the wider path it gave me a great thrill to see the huge footprints of a big hippopotamus that had passed that way not long before. We followed these until a trail of broken twigs and trampled grass to the left showed where he had turned his mighty bulk and slipped and slid down to the water's edge a hundred feet or more below. We walked to a lofty point which overlooks the Nile in both directions, giving a fine panoramic view of its first splendid sweep to the north, between high, wooded banks, an impressive sight. Then, partly retracing our steps, we made our way down to a rocky peninsula which juts out into the falls and enables one to come within touching distance of the great, green swirl of water that curls without a ripple over the edge of the first descent. The falls are really more cataracts than anything else, as the water rushes over an inclined plane of jagged rocks with little that could be called a fall.

A large colony of vultures were perched on the shores and boulders not far away. A little beyond them my guide pointed out the nostrils of several hippopotami who were lying close under the surface of the water; all that was visible of them being these breathing-holes — while across the rushing torrent his more practised eye also saw lying near a quiet pool a giant crocodile. To me it looked like some gnarled log. I dipped my hand in the rushing waters, which looked like molten beryl, to get the blessing of the Nile, and thought of the immense journey that the drops that slipped from my fingers were to take. Then we climbed the steep bank of red and slippery clay, and wended our way back to the house of my guide and host.

Here, being very warm and thirsty, we partook of the only alternative for whiskey and soda in this country, lime juice and lukewarm soda, ice being utterly unknown this side of Mombasa on the sea, and water being quite unattainable. We then inspected a very fine leopard cub, a beautiful spotted creature, whose hour of doom was drawing near. He was so large as soon to be getting dangerous, while even then he attracted wild leopards who came nightly snuffing around the house. Through the wooden bars of the box in which he was kept he looked like a splendid, dappled, golden cat. But one didn't care to caress him.

When we returned to the ship the air was already sneezingly redolent with the cargo of chillies we were shipping (the parent of cayenne pepper), a pungent, not disagreeable, but tickling odor.

Expressing great interest in the hippos of the lake, I was told that I was likely to hear the soft, musical, rather plaintive grunt of two or three which nightly haunted the harbor. So I tried to stay awake, but the lapping of the water against the ship's side was too soothing, and I soon fell asleep to be waked up by a small lemur, pet of one of the passengers, which jumped with its four clammy human paws full on my face. I knew instantly what it was, a most exquisite silky and gentle little beast, so the first shock passed, and after letting the creature curl up in a hollow at my feet, I again went to sleep, to awake only in the full, rosy flush of a tropical dawn.

The trip across the lake the next day was delightful. We were hardly ever out of sight of land. From the mainland or from the numerous islands that dot Victoria Nyanza we saw many clouds of the small insects known as the *kungu* fly, common to the lake district, rising in spirals, blown by the wind into what looked like waterspouts. Fortunately none drifted our way.

The painting of the benches was successfully finished. The monkey, which had escaped and fled to the most inaccessible part of the ship, was lured back by bananas, caught and secured. The lemur, which slept all day and prowled all night, was found curled up fast asleep in the captain's hat. For dinner we had once more a dish of that hot and excellent curry. Before sunset we came in sight of the wild, bare and lonely mountains which guard

Ripon Falls, Usoga Side

Beating Out Bark Cloth in Uganda

the entrance to Kavirondo Bay (called by some Kisumu Bay). As it was too near dark to be quite safe to navigate this bay, we anchored at its entrance, this making our third night on the *Sybil*. When we woke up the next morning we found ourselves moored alongside the clamorous dock at Port Florence, where stood the little train waiting for us and our luggage.

CHAPTER IX

THE JOURNEY CONTINUED

WITH the confusion which seems to attend all dealings with native porters, we had our belongings conveyed to the railway carriage and luggage van. Then, finding that there was still ample time before the starting hour — half-past eleven — to visit the Kavirondo market, a party of us decided to take in this one of the extraordinary sights of East Africa. As I have already said, the Kavirondos are the tribe living on the northeast shores of Lake Victoria, a tall, fine-looking, well-developed race, who are chiefly distinguished from the other East African tribes to be seen along the Uganda railway by the fact that the men and women, as a rule, wear absolutely no clothes, not even the customary loin-cloth. In spite of which they are said to be the most moral of the peoples of that region. They wear innumerable ornaments, however, of beads, gleaming copper wire, leather and elephant hair, which latter they twist into shiny, black bracelets and anklets. The copper wire they wind in heavy coils about their arms and legs. Their kinky, woolly locks are done in all sorts of fantastic styles, one gay and industrious buck having apparently strung every hair of his head full of glittering black beads, so that no hair was visible, only this rattling, shining, gorgon-like coiffure.

They also scarify themselves, having in connection with this some curious ideas. The women, to avert ill fortune from their husbands, cut vertical slits in their foreheads, making small scars. Or a devoted wife, to further propitiate fate, will make incisions in the skin of her abdomen, following a design, and by rubbing the juice of some plant in these will raise huge weals. My invaluable source of information in East Africa, Sir Harry Johnston, further writes that a Kavirondo husband before setting out to fight will make a few extra cuts in his wife's body " as a *porte-bonheur*."

They also, like their neighbors, the Masai and Nandi, have the custom of pulling out some of the lower teeth, usually the two middle incisors. Some one explains this habit among the Masai by saying that tetanus was once a scourge in East Africa and that it was found to be easy to feed a man suffering from lockjaw if there were gaps in his row of teeth. The explanation seems inadequate, as the custom is wide-spread among savages.

Leaving the steamer, we made our way across a bare, heat-bound stretch of ground to the native market. To the right in the distance were the houses of the European residents perched up above the lake. The place is said to be especially unhealthy, and it looks it, there being something depressingly dreary and miasmatic in the general aspect of it. The waters of Kavirondo Bay are not blue and fresh looking like those of Victoria Nyanza, but, owing to the presence of an enormous quantity of weeds and grasses, are brown and unwholesome in appearance.

The market was a large, open square, with a

roofed-over space in the middle, flanked on four sides with booths where the traders, Indian, Goanese and African, carried on their business. Under the central shelter little piles of seeds, millet, rice, corn, sesame, and many things with which I was not familiar, were ranged. There were unfamiliar fruits and what looked like mud pies. I never could find any one who knew what they were. And crowding every available place were ever-changing groups of these extraordinary savages. Seated on the ground, perhaps around a little fire, would be a circle of women, smoking queer pipes or cigarettes of native tobacco, or chewing nuts; while wandering about were bands of young warriors armed with strange shields and spears, or bows and arrows. Some were smeared with oil and plastered over with red mud. There was much ornamentation of the bodies of both men and women with curious designs pricked out with poison, which turned the flesh at each prick into a lump. The fine carriage of all these African savages was noticeable, due probably to the custom of carrying loads on their heads.

SOME AFRICAN HIGHWAYS

There were hundreds of these Kavirondos
wandering peaceably about, bartering for what
they wanted, using the strings of cowry shells
which in this part of Africa serve the natives
in lieu of money. At first they regarded us
with a shy, aloof interest, but after awhile were
inclined to too close an inspection for comfort,
and we left the enclosure, carrying with us
unforgettable mental pictures of human life in
its most primitive, elemental forms; dark,
glossy skins; tall, well-formed bodies; fine,
white teeth; soft, musical voices; beads of
many colors; shining copper-wire ornaments;
strange scarifications, and, finally, that pungent, unmistakable, suffocating African odor,
so suggestive of teeming, irrepressible, savage
life.

That afternoon, in the train, looking down a
steep slope, I saw a family of hyenas, high-
backed, hairy, hideous, tearing at some carrion,
probably left by a wandering lion.

At sunset, at Nakuru, a station in the Nandi
country, I got out to walk up and down during
the halt the train made there, and was much

Nubian Women Pounding Rice in Mortars Made of Tree Trunks

interested in the vast herds of cattle which the English had captured from the Nandis and driven in to the various stations. For the little Nandi war was now over, and the Nandis were suing for peace. As fast as the different divisions of the tribe would come in and give up their arms, their cattle would be returned to them, deducting a certain proportion for punishment. The sun was sinking in splendor, filling the wide plain which lies about Nakuru with a golden glory. The pens behind the station were filled with the lowing herds. The station platform was alive with native troops and good-looking English officers; and once more a recurring realization of the wonderful combination of firmly maintained order and wild and remote savagery swept over me. In how few years had this been achieved!

The train tooted and I mounted to our compartment, and in looking backward as we rumbled out caught one last glimpse of a wilderness of tossing horns against the gorgeous west   It was all that I saw of the Nandi war.

SOME AFRICAN HIGHWAYS

The Nandi and Masai are the most warlike among the East African tribes. This may be due to a custom common to both, that of drinking blood new-drawn, warm, and foaming from their oxen. The latter are bled by having a leather thong tied tightly around the throat. Below this bandage the warrior shoots an arrow into the neck, only just far enough to tap the vein. The arrow is drawn out and the blood gushing forth flows into earthen pots. When enough has been collected the thong is removed and the wound stopped up with a mixture of cow dung and dust. The frothing blood is sometimes mixed with sour or sweet milk, but is generally drunk alone, and supplies the salt necessary for the system.

We arranged ourselves as comfortably as we could for the night. We had not brought away with us the extra blankets with which we had provided ourselves on our upward journey, as we thought our travelling-rugs would be enough, and we did not wish to be encumbered with the heavy woollen things for the three weeks of tropical travel which lay before us. To supplement our steamer-rugs I had brought along a great armful of *Chicago Tribunes*. Paper is supposed to be a retainer of heat. Doubtless ours would have been if they had stayed on. But they spent the night slipping off. As we rose and crossed the eight thousand foot divide the air was thin and distressingly cold. I would swathe myself in those *Tribunes* and, after getting accustomed to their subdued crackle, would doze off, only to be awakened with a chill start by those wretched journals sliding off with a malicious, slithering rustle. It was what the French would call *une nuit penible*.

But dawn came at last, and I forgot the troubles of the night in my eagerness not to miss one instant of the wonderful Barnum's show which the Uganda Railway gives you. It is like a reversal of the usual circus procession. We were in the cages, moving through the land, while the animals we used to watch in their cages were now outside living their lives and gazing at us *en passant*. There was hardly a moment of the day when there was not in sight some interesting spectacle, either herds of zebras, or gnus, or gazelles of many kinds; or else three or four ostriches seesawing away; or a solitary secretary-bird with its fantastic crest; or a bald-headed vulture flying heavily from one low tree to another. Once more we came to Nairobi, the busy, bustling capital of British East Africa. Here some of our whilom steamer companions joined us to go down to Mombasa.

That afternoon came the two crowning experiences of our railway trip. I was playing a game of bridge under conditions sufficiently curious to be noted. My partner was a well-known English scientist, who had been sent out by the British government to investigate the sleeping-sickness. The other players were his wife, and one of the pioneers in East Africa, a man who has walked on foot from the sea to Uganda a half a dozen times, and is a great hunter of big game. Our table was a box built for a monkey, but which at that moment held only two giant sleeping tortoises, while the monkey sat on the professor's shoulder.

THE JOURNEY CONTINUED

The little lemur I mentioned as being on the boat was curled up inside the hat of madame, which she was wearing, while a gray parrot jabbered at us from a perch above. Outside the sun was declining in a golden haze when suddenly we saw five or six giraffes sidling off through some low trees. Their gait was as awkward as it is in the circus line of march, while their long necks seemed as much in the way as ever. Their dappled sides did not look so bright a gold as in the circus shows. Rather were they of a dun brown. They steered their small, frightened heads in and out of the upper branches of the scrub thorns, which grew here in ragged confusion, and soon slipped into the surrounding and protecting lights and shadows. Of all the wild creatures I saw in East Africa those giraffes impressed me the most. Their farouche heads, ridiculous necks, and shambling bodies seem so strangely unfamiliar and uncalled for.

Hardly had we got over this excitement and settled down to our game again — I had just made it " no trumps " — when we saw to the right of the track a huge lioness, bounding along not seventy feet away, keeping up easily with the train, which was proceeding in leisurely fashion. As she seemed so interested in us the train drew to a standstill, and at this the lioness crouched down in a little clump of grass, her great, powerful head and shoulders in full sight of all the passengers. The men in the train rushed to get out their guns. The excitement was intense with every one except the lioness. So agitated at the unexpected sight were the hunters that they could not find their ammunition. We had all got out on the steps of the train, and every eye was fixed on the dark form crouched eighty feet away. No one was frightened — though had the beast chosen she might have leaped on the crowd and dragged off a good supper, before the guns were ready. Much haste makes little speed, and before the ammunition turned up in a few minutes — it seemed much longer to the breathless onlookers — she turned, and, bounding deliberately across the track behind the train, disappeared in the bush. Bitterly disappointed, we

The Residence of the Commissioner at Entebbe

Governor's Palace at Dar Es Salaam

piled into the train again and continued our journey.

A little while later at dusk, a big lion, probably her mate, was seen on the other side of the track just before we pulled into the next station. This station, curiously enough, was Simba — the name meaning, as I have said before, "lion" — and was the scene of the famous lion story of East Africa. On the station platform lay the skin of a lion shot a day or so before. So plentiful are these creatures in that neighborhood that after nightfall those on one side of the track in the station never dare to cross to the few little shanties that lie on the other side twenty paces away. What became of our bridge game I don't know. But it is not often that a "no trump" hand is interrupted by a lion hunt.

We had three days to spend at Mombasa before the steamer came that was to take us down to South Africa. Such scorching, glaring days as those were — such suffocating nights! But the kindness and hospitality of the residents of Mombasa made the time go quickly.

SOME AFRICAN HIGHWAYS

We went several times to the club, a most attractive institution housed in a low, one-storied building, whose broad verandas, well furnished with deep lounging-chairs, look out across a most charmingly tropical garden — a space of coleas, palms, hibiscus, and other gorgeous shrubs — to the entrance of the harbor, a blue rippling strait with a veritable jungle of cocoanut and fibre palms on its further shore, dense, impenetrable, mysterious looking. Here we had tea or iced drinks, and the ice *was* a luxury! During my stay in Entebbe I planned to make my everlasting fortune by running jointly an ice machine and a laundry. As there would be no other competitors in the field, my ice business would practically be a monopoly and I could charge what I liked after I had developed the taste for it in the Entebbeans. While the water not used in ice, or which would otherwise be lost by the melting ice, could be employed in a laundry. The present method for the latter is a sort of dry wash; the clothes are soaped and then pounded on a box or an inverted tin tub. Then,

to judge from the results, they are torn " limb
from limb " — " mangled " the process is called,
and it is well named. Tattered remnants were
all we rescued from the Entebbean clothes-
washers. The boys who do the laundry work
are called *dhobi* boys — and are able to
gauge their work so well that a small wash
takes quite as long as a large one.

One of the warm evenings at Mombasa we
went in a rumbling little trolley to dine with
hospitable Mrs. E. It was delicious riding
bareheaded and bare-necked through the darkness, the smelly lantern at our feet casting a
pale circle of light on the little rails, which
fairly whizzed under the swift rush of our
trolley-boys. When we came to a descent the
boys would cling on to the sides of the trolley
and coast down. The heavy odor of frangipani
filled the night. Lights gleamed out of low
windows of distant bungalows.

The company was delightful, the dinner
excellent, and very well served by the number-
less barefooted boys, one of whom sat outside
and pulled the string of the big punkah over

our heads. The room was high and airy, with some native spears and shields ornamenting the walls.

Another day we rumbled over at noon to lunch with Mrs. D. The meal was served in a wide, breezy upper veranda enclosed in lattice. It was most refreshing, after the glaring heat outside that sizzled up from the white coral sands and beat against the face in oppressive waves, to step into the cool shade of that spacious balcony. There was much good cheer and interesting talk.

On a bright, but not too warm, afternoon, Judge H. took us in a smart little rowboat to Freretown, the missionary station on the mainland. It was an orderly, well-kept place, where the natives were neatly clad in European garb. This seems a pity, as besides taking from them all individuality, it is said to make them prone to European maladies.

The place is named for Sir Bartle Frere, in honor of his memorable visit to Zanzibar to induce Seyyid Bargash to suppress the slave-trade. To England belongs the entire credit for the extinction of this infamous traffic, called out there " the Middle Passage." That it still flourishes in West Africa is the darkest blot on modern civilization.

At Freretown we saw the very fine church entirely built by the natives. We also visited a melancholy little cemetery where the riotous fervor of tropical vegetation is trying to hide and obliterate the gray slabs inscribed with the names of those who died far from home. The whole place left a sad impression of fruitless struggle, of forces too strong for the power brought to fight them. Remove the settlement and in less than a year the converts would revert to savagery, and the rank, tropical vegetation would run riot in their neat enclosures, and not one trace of the labor of the missionaries would remain in the heart of the people or on the face of the land. The sombre power of Africa to remain African in spite of European invasion is unmistakable. The white intruders do not look at home under the heavy mango-trees, or suitable to the landscape of palms and bananas. They may build their railroads and establish their families in the Dark Continent, but they continue to be aliens. They merely scratch the surface of Africa, whose own dusky children remain at heart savage and apart, while the wilderness is always lurking close at hand ready to reclaim any piece of cultivated ground and strangle it in its own lush growth.

CHAPTER X

TO DAR ES SALAAM

A T noon, in a fervid and glittering intermission between heavy tropical showers, we
steamed out of the inner harbor of Mombasa, on
the Kilindini side of the island. The well-buoyed
channel led us past the low green point where,
perched high to catch every sea breeze, stood
the hospitable bungalows we knew so well
by now. On the opposite side stretched the
long spit of mainland, where the dense jungle
of palms and other tropic foliage so vividly
recalled Robinson Crusoe and kindred romances.
Outside this, in a vast semicircle, the Indian
Ocean showed its cruel, white teeth, as its waters
broke over the enclosing coral reefs.

Our first stop was at Tanga, a port in German
East Africa. As it was night by the time we
were swinging about on our anchor, we did not

go ashore, but took a moonlight row in the almost landlocked harbor. These sparkling waters are said to be uncommonly full of sharks, so we were more than usually careful not to capsize. Except that the moon was larger, fuller, more radiant than usual, while the air was peculiarly balmy, and freighted with strange, spicy land smells, we might have been bobbing about a moonlight night on Lake Michigan. What we could see of the shores showed them to be low and wooded. The next morning before sun-up we were away to Zanzibar.

Zanzibar — doesn't the name call up tales of the Arab slave-trading days? Didn't our geographies tell us that the chief exports of this ancient and tropical isle were cloves and copra? Isn't there a Sultan of Zanzibar famous in song? It is far stranger, more mysterious and fascinating than any song or geography or romance gives any idea of, but this time we were not allowed to land, because of plague there and of quarantine regulations at other ports. It was on our return journey that we had our glimpse of Zanzibar. So, regretfully we gazed across the intensely green-blue waters at the sea-front of the city, with its quaint Arab houses and minarets rising in picturesque confusion. In the centre of the picture stands the Sultan's palace with its tier on tier of iron verandas, running across each story of its new, garish front; the whole looking more like an unsightly American watering-place hotel than an Oriental potentate's palace. His predecessor had a very effective and historic-looking dwelling some ten years ago, but this was shelled by the English at a critical moment. At that time Germany claimed suzerainty over Zanzibar. The German emperor concluded that in his scheme of military establishment, the rocky, bleak, uninhabitable island of Heligoland in the Baltic would be of more use to him than his rather uncertain control of Zanzibar, so he bartered with Great Britain, exchanging his somewhat hazy claims on the East African isle for the rock in the Baltic. There are few German travellers on the East Coast who do not to-day regret this exchange, for the island is one of the richest and most productive in the world.

On the conclusion of the treaty the English admiral nearest at hand (his name I've forgotten) was ordered to sail into the harbor of Zanzibar and hoist the British flag. The Sultan of Zanzibar, however, objected to the transaction all around, and manned a silly, ineffectual little ship with some silly and ineffectual little men and sent it out in the bay to meet the mightiest sea power in the world. It is rather a pathetic picture. The British admiral promptly sank the foolish craft with all on board and then shelled the palace. It was said that there were a good many women and children in it at the time, but this does not seem probable. The whole war was over in an hour; the Sultan was a fugitive on a German man-of-war and the English were full masters of the most desirable port on the East Coast. The masts and spars of the miserable little ship still stick up out of the rippling waters of the bay, a favorite roosting-place for gulls. The ruins of the palace have been removed and a

Scene in Zanzibar

A Street in Zanzibar

distant relative of the Sultan established on his throne, an empty honor at the best. The dethroned ruler was taken to German East Africa, where he was pensioned and kindly treated. I think he still lives there. If not, he died only recently.

There is a rule in the British navy — I presume we have a similar one in ours — that no officer lower in rank than an admiral may take his wife or womenkind in his ship for a cruise, but an admiral may. This particular one happened to have both his wife and daughter on board when he was obliged to bombard Zanzibar. As there was nowhere to land them, they had the unusual experience for women of being on board a man-of-war when it was in action.

It is only a few hours' trip from Zanzibar to Dar Es Salaam. The sun was half-way to the western horizon when we steamed into the large, entirely landlocked harbor of the capital of German East Africa, which is reached by a very narrow, winding channel. The town lies in a wide semicircle on the shores of the bay, the steeples of the ·two churches — the Catholic and German Lutheran — standing like exclamation-points against the sky-line.

As soon as our anchor was dropped our attention was called to a very trim-looking rowboat, manned by dusky sailor lads in white sailor suits, trimmed with blue, which put out from a very pretty, white-balustraded pier, and darted towards us. A uniformed young German officer sat erect in the stern, and the red, white, and black flag of the fatherland trailed behind him. It was the cutter of the governor, sent by his wife to convey us and our luggage to her house; for we were fortunate enough to be invited by the charming Countess von Goetzen to visit her during the time the ship lay in harbor. As we were carrying an unusually large cargo of steel rails for the new German railroad up into the interior, we had five very delightful days there while these rails were unloaded.

Count Adolf von Goetzen had been at the head of German affairs in this part of the world

since 1901, and under his administration won-
ders have been accomplished. Fine roads have
been laid out in all directions; pretty new houses,
up-to-date in every particular, have been built
for the officials, with bricks and tiles brought
from Germany, while the native quarter is a
model of cleanly orderliness. Much as I admire
English colonial methods, I must admit that
in Dar Es Salaam the Germans have out-
stripped their neighbors in some directions, and
their intense energy, industry and zeal are a
marked contrast to the more deliberate and
conservative methods which sometimes char-
acterize British officials in the tropics. To be
sure, they have put an enormous amount of
money into the making of this the capital of
German East Africa, and their British neighbors
say that England does not put money into a
place unless she sees a sure and not too far off
return for it, while the Germans are looking
to the very remote future for their return on
the millions that annually go to the support
and development of this colony.

The governor's house is a veritable palace

out of the Arabian Nights Tales, set in the loveliest tropical garden I ever saw, a park of palms, gorgeous shrubs, giant ferns, and fragrant with frangipani, champak, and other sweet or spicy flowers. On one side one descends by broad terraces to the sea, where there is a skirting path under a row of pale, shimmering African hemlocks. The main approach to the house is by a straight, densely shaded avenue of mango-trees. The residence is a vast, square, white-stuccoed structure with an overhanging roof, and a huge encircling two-storied veranda, whose double tier of Moorish arches and pillars gives the house its romantic character.

On either side of the imposing doors, as we entered through files of sentries and white-gowned native servants, were two guest-rooms, big, airy apartments, most exquisitely furnished. Further on was the great square hall, unroofed and open to the blue sky. In the centre was a fine bronze bust of the emperor on a marble pedestal. The walls were ornamented with spears and shields and native trophies. At one side on a low platform stood an elephant in ebony, with ivory tusks, surrounded by little elephants of the same make, the big one being about four feet tall, a piece of fine and imposing workmanship. Opposite the entrance were the offices of the governor, and a pretty reception-room which opened out on a charming terrace overlooking the sea, where every afternoon the countess received guests and dispensed tea. A fine wide staircase leads to the upper and main story, where were the apartments of the count and countess; the dining-room and drawing-rooms, all beautifully furnished with the taste which especially distinguished Countess von Goetzen. Heavily carved teak-wood furniture, softly shaded lamps, rich Oriental coverings and draperies, a profusion of silver vases full of flowers, photographs, framed and unframed, and choice knickknacks gave an air of sumptuous finish quite bewildering when you considered where you were. These rooms all opened out by many French windows to the wide, shady verandas, where were wicker chairs, couches and tables and big grass-woven mats. By day, when the glare might be disagreeable, soft, green reed curtains shut out the light and let in the breezes; by night, however, these were raised and the scene, as one looked out into the rustling palms, baobabs, mango-trees and other tropical foliage, was magical, whether seen by the dazzling moon (which almost glares in the tropics) or by the wonderful starlight.

On the two main fronts of the house this upper veranda widened out to great open-air apartments. In one of these, on especially stifling evenings, the big round dinner-table was sometimes laid with, as the society reporter would put it, " covers " for twenty or thirty. With its glittering crystal and silver, its charming garlands of the flame-of-the-forest (an exquisite tropical blossom) and its shaded candles, it made a beautiful oasis of light in the shadows of an East African night. The livery of the countess's household was the most effective I saw in that part of the world. In addition to the embroidered cap and long white gown, or *kanzu*, the servants wore black zouave jackets richly embroidered in gold, and were girt with red, fringed sashes, tied at the side. An infinite number of them flitted noiselessly about in the service of the house. This prodigality of attendance is very demoralizing to one used to the more austere system of self-help in America. In East Africa no one ever lifts his finger for even the smallest service. To move a chair, to pick up a card, to open a door, to lift a book, a boy is called, in fact, is generally close at hand. And most of these servants were born savages in grass huts, of people who hunted with bows and arrows, and occasionally enjoyed a little cannibalistic feast.

The Germans have trained their natives wonderfully, those that they have adapted to their civic and domestic usages. The first morning after our arrival we were serenaded by the native band of some twenty-five or thirty pieces. There they stood outside our windows clad in regimentals (stiff khaki helmets, neat coats and knee-breeches of the same, and shiny, bare black legs) around their leader, a German in full uniform. The music was excellent, given with spirit and precision. The

German, with the indomitable perseverance of his race, had trained them, he speaking not one word of their language, they not one word of his. Each man had had to be separately taught his instrument. Probably none of them could read any written language, yet each could read his little sheet of music, and tune his instrument, and play in accord with his fellows. It was a sight worth seeing, and a serenade worth listening to, there in the shade of those thick, black trees, with the foreground of dazzling, white coral-sand road, the intense blue sky above and the sentries who walked up and down a few feet from our windows all day and all night.

Down by the sea, at the end of that pleasant walk under the feathery hemlocks, was the aquarium, one of the most fascinating and interesting sights in all of East Africa. It was the especial hobby of Count von Goetzen. Housed in a most artistic little white stucco building, with its feet really in the sea, stands this young, audacious rival of the far-famed Naples aquarium. On entering we descended about ten steps and found ourselves in a space of cool, shimmering, green shadows, as the light came from above through the glass tanks on either side. And in these tanks floated, or cosily slumbered, the strangest, weirdest denizens of the Indian Ocean; horrid mottled octopi; grewsome, pallid sea-worms, of huge size; little fishes of most opalescent transparency; other strange fishes that seemed to be trailing brown and white feathers, instead of fins; still others that looked like abortive birds of the swallow variety. It was truly a wonderful assortment, living in bosky dells of seaweed and sea-anemones and queer shells and coral formations that must often have cheated them into forgetting their captivity. On a later visit the count told me of a curious battle that took place in one of the tanks where the sea-worm and a huge octopus dwelt in apparent amity till the day the adventure befell. It was a great relaxation for the count to take an hour or so in his very busy life to watch the creatures in the aquarium. Noticing one day that the pale sea-worm was not visible he hunted for him, and discovered all that was left of him was a still struggling end — tail or head, who can tell? — sticking out of the swollen mouth of the monstrous octopus, who was evidently struggling internally with the rest. Soon even the last wriggling remnant disappeared, though the struggle seemed still to go on for some time inside.

Count von Goetzen in his youth made a remarkable journey through the unexplored interior of Africa. On this occasion he was the discoverer of an active volcano. He wrote an interesting and valuable book describing this expedition.

His wife, who is a beautiful woman, is, as I have stated elsewhere, an American, and is profoundly interested in all her husband's plans for and work in East Africa. She is of great assistance to him by the charming way in which she administers their truly beautiful home and dispenses a hospitality that makes Dar Es Salaam famous on the East Coast.[1]

[1] Since writing the above, the count has returned to Germany, his health shattered by his arduous labors in German East Africa.

A Mother and Child

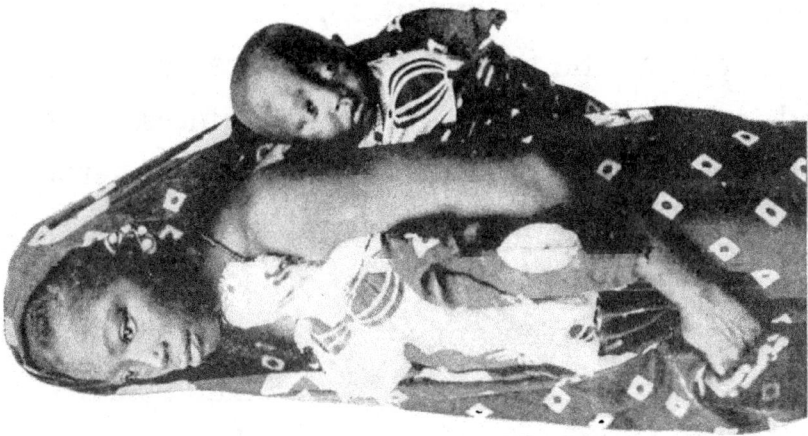

Swahili Girl

TO DAR ES SALAAM

One of the many interesting things I saw in Dar Es Salaam was what they call a " zebride," a cross between a zebra and a horse. This was a young, sturdy-looking colt, gamboling about with its zebra mother, the latter quite as frisky as her offspring. The stripes, so striking in her coat, were only faintly visible on his gray sides. His sire was evident in the lines of his head and withers. His maternal ancestry was clearly to be traced in his stocky flanks and rather barrel-like body.

As horses are very difficult to raise and keep in that part of the world, if a workable animal could be evolved from the horse and the zebra, which is indigenous, it would be a most useful and valuable evolution.

In spite of the fact that horses are both frail and costly in tropical Africa, Countess von Goetzen had a smart-looking mail phaeton drawn by two pretty cream-colored horses, and there were a good many other neat traps to be seen any pleasant afternoon tooling over the fine, hard roads; roads bordered and shaded by palms or mango-trees, or by the gorgeous

" flamboyant," whose crimson, bell-shaped blossoms make a flaming mass of color. One of the prettiest drives is that under the feathery hemlocks along by the sea, with the waves lapping the sands not twenty feet away, while the intervening beach is alive and rustling with myriads of spider-like crabs, scampering sideways with incredible swiftness. These drives are the more noteworthy as in the neighboring colonies the residents use only rickshaws or trolleys.

Through all my memories of German East Africa — among the pleasantest of our trip — comes the odor of some tropical flowering shrub — pungent, aromatic, rather like chillies — that grew outside of our windows; and a vivid sensation of the all-pervading, soaking, suffocating heat; a heat that permeated the brilliant days — except for the few hours of the afternoon sea breeze — and drenched the velvety, fragrant, tropical nights so that when we arose in the morning we left the damp outline of our sleeping selves on our couches.

The impression this German colony left on

me was of an intensely energetic, ambitious community, whose overmastering desire is to outdo the English in their hitherto undisputed field as the world's chief colonizers; an ambition the English do not yet quite realize or recognize. The latter, having for so long been *facile princeps* in this line, are now a little apt to take it easy, to rest on their laurels, unwitting of the competitor who is straining every nerve and every resource to pass them on the road. With the German official his work is the first and only consideration. With the Englishman all over the world his recreation and sport are a close second in importance to his official duties. This is a serious element of weakness and one that might in time lose this people their place in the van of the procession. As yet, however, they belong there at the head, as no other nation brings such a kindliness, tolerance, and sense of justice to the problem of handling inferior races. The British official also unites to his undeniable ability and wide experience a sense of honor that is incorruptible.

But all these five charming days when we

were so delightfully entertained on shore, our ship, the *Kronprinz*, lay out in the harbor, the windlasses creaking and screeching all but three out of the twenty-four hours, the iron rails clanging and banging with incredible clamor on their journey from the hold to the lighters moored alongside. For those of the passengers who stayed on board ship the time was a distressing wait. At length the cargo was delivered, we returned to our cabins, and it was up anchor and away to Mozambique!

As we steamed out into the Indian Ocean we got one last glimpse of the governor's palace. Like a vision it stood, gleaming white, embowered in palms, while near it on the shore the exquisite aquarium nestled at the end of the hemlock walk. Looking back a few minutes after leaving it, it was impossible to distinguish the entrance to Dar Es Salaam harbor, so enclosed is it in headlands and islands.

CHAPTER XI

FROM EAST TO SOUTH AFRICA

THE five days that we had been lying in the tranquil landlocked harbor of Dar Es Salaam a lively hurricane had been rousing up the Indian Ocean, strewing the shores of the islands and mainland down towards Mozambique with wrecks, so that when at length we turned southward we found ourselves in the tail end of this storm — and the tail was still wagging. Though the skies were clear the sea was piled high with great, pale green waves up which we climbed and down which we slid till we anchored in the harbor of Mozambique. Even here it was too rough to go ashore in the little boats, so we gazed at the ancient, cream-colored fortress (built by the Portuguese in the time of the redoubtable Vasco da Gama, who discovered and settled Mozambique) and noted the gay colors of the neat-looking buildings on the water-front, red, blue and every tone of yellow, and in a few hours steamed out and away for Beira.

Seven years ago, when the railway to Salisbury was being built, Beira was an important, hustling, bustling port of entry. Tin huts sprouted in a night like white-ant mushrooms. Even some very nice houses were put up. A veritable boom in real estate took place, and, when you consider that nearly every other shanty was a saloon, and that all did a brisk business, you can get some idea of the cheerful tone that prevailed. To-day, the railway being finished, the boom has collapsed. The Portuguese government has placed such heavy duties on both incoming and outgoing goods that it is said Rhodesia is more cheaply reached via Cape Town. This has stifled commerce. The doors of the shanties hang open, creaking on rusty hinges. The decent houses go a-begging for tenants. The saloons still flourish, but not with their former *éclat*. A man who drinks from despondency is never so exhilarating as he who imbibes with high hopes. And the sand on which the town is laid out, that shifting, impenetrable, inexhaustible medium, is fast creeping, blowing, drifting up to swallow and hide the pitiful evidences of failure and collapse.

It was Christmastide when we were there, though in Beira there was no evidence of the season. The heat was intense, glaring, unremitting. No church was to be seen; there were no signs of festivity. A steaming apathy pervaded the land and even crept across the brassy waters to our ship, lying in solitary state in the harbor, unloading a slim cargo for the interior country. But Christmas is the chief festival of the year to Germans, and so the *Kronprinz*, sailing under the red, white and black flag, celebrated it in due form. A gay Christmas tree, — brought out for the purpose from the fatherland, — a souvenir for each guest, speeches and toasts made the dining-saloon an oasis of cheer in as un-Christmassy a spot as could be found on the broad earth's surface that night.

The sea had subsided by the time we steamed

out and away for Lorenco Marques, the principal port in Portuguese East Africa. Unlike Beira, Lorenco Marques has thriven and grown in the last six years, being the nearest seaport to the Transvaal and having received a big impetus at the time of the Boer war. Delagoa Bay, on which the town is situated, is a fine harbor, and docks have been built alongside of which even the largest ships can unload. The sanitary condition of the place — once notoriously bad — has been much improved. Pretty houses in well-kept gardens now stretch out to the point where stands the lighthouse. The roads are good. An excellent system of electric trams enables one to go all over the place. The Portuguese currency is so divided into infinitesimal fractions that even a short ride costs an enormous number of *res*. For a circuit of the town I believe we paid nearly 2,000 *res*. A glass of lemonade taken outside of one of the little kiosks, on the sunbaked, principal square, cost another 500 *res*. As we sat there ladies in diaphanous gowns, carrying gay parasols, fluttered by in rickshaws drawn by steaming natives. Portuguese officers, undersized, but important looking, strolled about. Residents, and passengers from the steamers lying in harbor, walked up and down in pith helmets and light-colored clothes, for it was very, *very* warm. In the flower beds that dotted the white square, poinsettias, hibiscus, and other tropical shrubs flaunted their gorgeous hues. Not a breath of air came to us from the glassy harbor, where with much creaking of cranes and shouts and shrill steam whistles, a half a dozen steamers were unloading their various cargoes. It was with a gasp of relief that we departed by the night train for Johannesburg. We had a most comfortable compartment in a very well-finished car, while an excellent dining-car gave us good *a la carte* meals the next day.

It was an hour after sunset and we could see little of the country as we pulled out of Lorenco Marques. A gigantic crescent moon was sinking low on the western horizon and shone across a flat, marshy land, thickly sprinkled with thorn bushes. Whenever we stopped at the lonely, infrequent little stations, a shrill chorus of frogs filled the night, while hot, damp odors were wafted in from the dreary, untenanted waste.

We roused ourselves at early dawn the following morning to look out at the wild, weird, misty mountains that mark a remarkable ascent to the high veldt at a place called " Waterfallboven." Great, bare, rounded peaks, wreathed in trailing mists, towered in chaos on every side. The air was nipping and eager. In an incredibly short time we rose nearly six thousand feet to the vast plain of Central South Africa. We were in the Transvaal, and from this point to Johannesburg the route was marked by block-houses, many of which, shattered by shells, were roofless ruins, dreary mementoes of war. Although the high veldt is supposed to be an immense level plain, it is in reality a very broken plateau. In parts steep kopjes rise in every direction, while in other parts the land rolls in huge undulations of treeless green. The peculiarity of the South African kopje is that it seems to be a creation

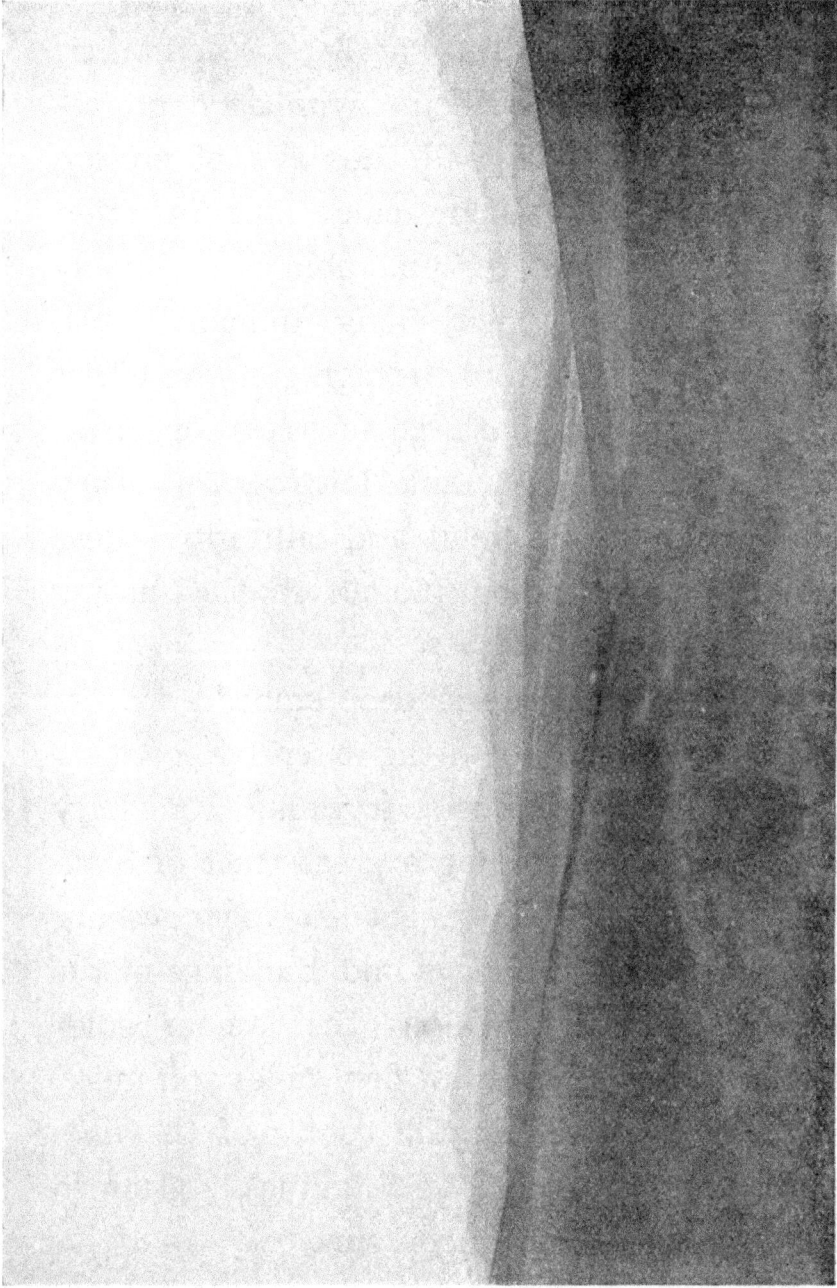

Typical View of the High Veldt

of caprice. No two run parallel to each other. They sprout up without symmetry or co-relation, disregarding all the laws of erosion or construction which make hills in other lands into ranges. Innumerable birds, glossy black of plumage, with long, unmanageable, waving tails, rose from the high grass on either side of the track, fluttered in uncertain, awk-ward flight and then sank down again. They are peculiar to the veldt and only grow these trailing, incommoding plumes in the mating season.

As we passed Pretoria, deep embedded in its heavy foliage, we noted the extensive fortifica-tions built by the Boers, frowning from lofty kopjes and commanding a great tract of terri-tory. Long before we got to Johannesburg we saw the tall chimneys and buildings of the mines which stretch along the famous gold-bearing reef, or Rand, for fifty miles and more, with Johannesburg in the centre of the line; while the huge piles of " tailings " gleamed like snow in the afternoon sun.

It was quite exciting to be once more in a big

and bustling city. As my brother's automobile whisked us from the station to his home on Hospital Hill, overlooking the town, it seemed to me that I had never before seen so many people or so many vehicles hurrying here and there. As we cut around corners, at what seemed to us — used to the more leisurely gharries and trolleys of East Africa — a fearful speed, I held on to my seat and my hat with a fear greater than any I had known in face of lions or other perils in the tropics.

Johannesburg has changed very much in character and tone since the days of the Boer *régime*. The old, easy-going spirit of prosperity and high hope is gone. The people are restless, discontented and much inclined to despond. They must sometimes feel as if they had exchanged King Log for King Stork. The Boer officials were a corruptible, untrustworthy lot, no doubt, while the English officials are just the contrary; but they are as numerous as were the locusts in Egypt. There are said to be one for every four inhabitants of the country. Of course a people so ridden with officialdom becomes irritated, impatient, exhausted. But all the depression which at present is the prevailing tone there cannot be laid to this. The mines have been over-capitalized. In order to work them to sufficient profit to support this heavy financial burden the mine-owners must have cheap labor. The Kaffirs cannot be induced to return in sufficient numbers to operate the mines, so Chinese labor has been imported. In many ways this is detrimental to the country at large. They are a menace to public safety. They take out of the country much of the money they earn; and, since the time of the Helots in Greece, it has never been found to the advantage of any nation to have its tasks done by outsiders. Those not directly interested in the mines are vigorously protesting against this importation. The mine-owners are as strenuous in maintaining their position, even threatening to close every mine on the Rand. Downing Street, ten thousand miles away, is prone to irritate both parties to the controversy by tactless interference, and the result is a state of seething discontent and a depression which spreads from the financial to the social life. The clear warm sun and the bracing winds of the high veldt shine and blow on a distracted, unhappy community of people gathered from all quarters of the globe, for Johannesburg is essentially cosmopolitan. Americans, Germans, Dutch, Italian, French, Scandinavians, all mingle in the life there with the English and Boers. While the chosen people are so thick that the town is often called Jew-hannesburg.

The centre of the city is the huge market-place, flanked at one end by the big post-office. On this dusty square congregate on certain days of the week the Boer farmers of the outlying district, who, as they express it, *trek* into town with their big, slow teams of oxen, to exchange their produce for various commodities. They make quaint and picturesque groups. The place always swarms with Kaffirs, generally clustered about some Jew auctioneer, who is selling off old, suspicious-looking beds, and other unsavory truck to eager bidders. The South African Kaffir is very different from the

Central African negro, both physically and mentally. Modified by climate and by the fact that food is not to be had for the picking, he is of a more stalwart build and more energetic disposition. Rightly handled much work can be got out of him. He is as a rule tall, well made, and a chocolate brown in color. But the savage is close under the skin, in spite of over a hundred years of white dominion. The rickshaw-boys of Johannesburg delight to deck themselves out in most fantastic attire. Feathers in their hair, waving skirts of many hued, fringed tissue-paper, rows of jingling bells on their bare legs, and a lot of other queer devices are the means they employ to attract attention. There is a curious convention about the use of rickshaws. Whereas in Johannesburg it is not at all " the thing " to ride in them, it is the universal custom in Durban and in all East African towns. But this may be because cabs are plentiful and comparatively cheap in Johannesburg and not in the other places.

The principal business highway, Commissioner Street, is lined with fine office buildings, those of the older types having arcades over the sidewalks, which make a pleasant shade in the fierce African sunlight.

To the north and east of the city the favorite residence portions are situated on overlooking heights. Here is to be found every style of dwelling, from the low, cosy, one-storied bungalow, to the Elizabethan mansion, all being set in charming gardens, bright with flowers and enclosed with high green hedges. The most desirable residence portion, Parktown, has an amazing number of really beautiful houses, which have all been built since the war. Of imposing architecture, they are perched on splendid sites overlooking the wide, wonderful stretch of country northward towards Pretoria.

The mine-owners have planted in different directions vast groves, or plantations of Australian gum-trees, eucalyptus, and other quick-growing trees to provide timber for the mine shafts. Roads wind through these and give delightful, shady drives to the Jo'burgers (for, with an American tendency to brevity, the name is often so shortened). The roads are the rich African red clay. The woods are of all shades of green from the silver shimmering gray of the young gum-trees to the dense black of pines.

Through unexpected openings one's breath is taken away by distant vistas of the wide, sunny veldt gleaming with all the gorgeous colors of noon or sunset. To skim through these wooded glades in one of the swift automobiles — of which there seem to be thousands — and then to dash out across the breezy veldt is one of the chief pleasures of the place. The air is always intoxicating, the altitude, 5,700 feet, causing this, and the wonderful sense of space and freedom, with the great dome of sky overhead, cannot fail to be exhilarating.

But the spirit of the place is wrong. An exclusively money-seeking community cannot develop any fine tone. On the one hand the mine-owners are seeking to foster their industry at the expense of the country, while on the other the British government is hampering and weighing it down with a cumbersome officialdom most exasperating to the many alien elements struggling to make a living there. The problem will doubtless work itself out through the right to self-government which has now been given the country, which right may foster a public spirit and disinterested affection for the place now utterly lacking. But there are many dark days ahead of this once brilliant community before it shall stand on its feet on solid ground. That it will do so seems beyond a doubt, though it is to be hoped that the old feverish days of boom and speculation will never return.

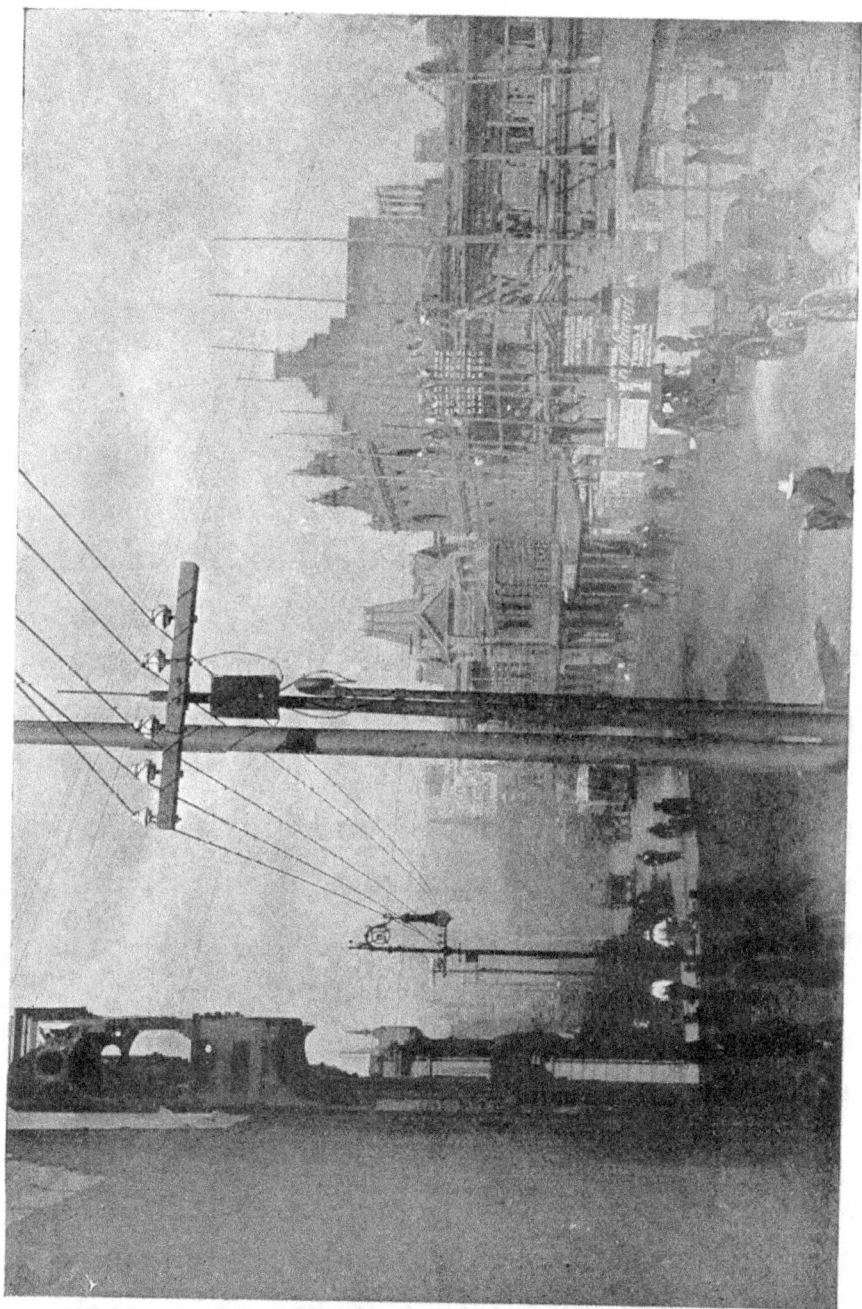

Dust Storm in Commissioner Street, Johannesburg

CHAPTER XII

THE RAND CHINESE

HAVING expressed a desire to see the much-talked of Chinese mine-workers, we were taken one day to the Simmer and Jack, one of the most important of the Rand mines, employing I don't know how many thousands of celestials. The compound where they were housed, fed and cared for generally was a huge enclosure containing many buildings, comprising kitchens, living-rooms, sleeping quarters, hospital, and offices for those in charge of this alien labor.

On the way to the mine, whither we went in a motor, we passed straggling groups of Chinese, the most forbidding, uncanny gathering of mortals I have ever seen. Their attire and general get-up would have been ludicrously fantastic had it not been for the soulless, sinister human masks that looked at us with gleaming, glancing, slanting eyes. The types were astonishing, both in number and variety, but all had one characteristic expression — namely, inscrutability. Fat, sleek-faced coolies from South China mingled with gaunt specimens from the north, where they bear a close resemblance to the Russian Cossack, or Calmuck. The dress was wonderful in its infinite variety, and extraordinary mingling of colors and fashions. But the effect was rather appalling in its suggestion of a fateful race of whose potentialities the rest of the world knows so little.

It is the wandering bands who have run away from their respective mines that terrorize the outlying country about Johannesburg, pillaging, burning and attacking defenceless residents, so that many a lonely household has had to break up and send the women and children to the town, while the men of the family look out for themselves.

The Chinese, however, that we saw in the Simmer and Jack compound seemed a quiet, orderly, biddable lot, while their quarters and food must have been far better and cleaner than anything they had ever known in any previous condition of life. In the big kitchens huge caldrons of soup and of rice bubbled on the fires, while the long tables were piled high with meats and fresh vegetables being prepared in most appetizing messes. There were also kitchens set apart where they could do their own cooking, and we saw many making delicious looking pastries and patties for themselves. In the sleeping-quarters were built rows of low platforms, each Chinaman having a little square space to himself, generally enclosed by curtains of some flowered print, or cheap white stuff. In the enclosures were gathered a curious collection of treasures; perhaps a Buddha, or Chinese god enshrined with fancy picture cards or tinsel, or a paltry something made in Birmingham. Everything was clean, airy and sanitary. The charge of ill-treatment or slavery falls flat when confronted with existing conditions. The dangers in the experiment lie entirely outside the compound, and menace the country, not the aliens imported into it.

SOME AFRICAN HIGHWAYS

In the operation of most of the mines of the famous Witwatersrand (White-water reef) the task is curiously divided among four great nationalities. The English own them; the Jews finance them; as a rule the engineering corps is composed of Americans; while the manual labor is done by Chinese. Of course there are exceptions. Some of the mines are worked by Kaffirs, and some have English or German engineers; while some of the active financiers are of various nationalities. But the above is the usual and very characteristic division of labor. Most of the American engineers are Californians, or have had their early training in the mines out in the western part of our country. This makes an important colony of Americans in Johannesburg. An energetic and forceful element they are, meddling little actively in politics, but indirectly influencing the community in the direction of absolute local freedom, and in no small degree responsible for the intolerance of outside interference which characterizes the place. Probably in none of the British dependencies is there so much dis-

Typical Mine Buildings at Johannesburg

affection as in South Africa. England holds these colonies by a very frail thread. When the controversy as to the employment of Chinese labor was most acute and the home government — the newly arrived liberal party — issued the statement that it would forthwith stop any further importation of Chinese, both sides to the dispute in the Transvaal promptly joined forces and vehemently protested against such unwarranted interference. Far more important than any industrial problem was the question of their right to manage their own affairs. Again, when, a month or so later, the same government forbade the execution of some native rebels in Natal, the whole of South Africa rose in protest. The Natal ministry resigned, and from Rhodesia to the Cape the country seethed with rage. The officials in England had finally to recede from their stand.

The present governor of the Transvaal and Orange River Colonies, the successor to Lord Milner, is Lord Selborne, who has proved himself a *persona grata* to the conflicting elements.

Lord Milner did excellently in the days when
war was rending the land. He had a firm hand
and a dogged tenacity of purpose. But when
peace descended and tact and conciliation
became necessary he was found wanting. He
is a German by birth and early training and
the stubborn Teuton in him would not adapt
itself to altered conditions. His going was
almost as welcome as his coming had been.

Lord Selborne is a typical Britisher, upright,
serene, with a keen sense of justice, not very
quick or brilliant, but an excellent man to win
the respect and confidence of all parties. His
wife, who is a daughter of the late Marquis
of Salisbury and therefore one of the famous
Cecil family, has done much to raise the tone
of social life in Johannesburg. Under the
preceding *régime*, with its bachelor chief, the
social standard was not very high. Undesirable
elements crept into undesirable notoriety, but
Lady Selborne's gracious firmness and tact
are altering all this.

Looking back on Johannesburg, I find that
it left an impression of dust and sunshine,

smartly dressed people whizzing about in automobiles, on broad, straight streets; up long, steep hills, with glimpses of pretty homes in lovely gardens on either hand, while ever and anon came flashes of the gorgeous veldt at street ends; that great, broad bosom of mother earth that cradles so genially the most materialistic and money-seeking community in the world. The savage solitudes of Central Africa are in some ways preferable to this to one not hunting for gold, and it was with small regret that we left Jo'burg and turned once more northward via Lorenco Marques and the wonderful East Coast.

Our passage had been taken in one of the first-class ships of the German line that controls most of the traffic on the East Coast. But at that time the Duke of Connaught, who was making a semi-royal tour of South Africa, announced his intention of returning home by this line and route the following month. As the steamer which should have sailed at the date he selected was one of the smaller, less desirable ones, the company, with a laudable desire to accommodate royalty, detained and substituted the boat we had expected to take, and put in its place a small, ignoble craft, which was taken off what is called the intermediate or second-class line, an act of doubtful business honor, as no refund was made to those who, having paid for good accommodations, were forced to take bad ones.

We spent thirty-three days on this 3,400-tonner, and experienced all the vicissitudes of primitive travel. There was no ice machine or cold storage room, so all our meat was carried alive on the forward deck and killed as required. As this deck also carried the motley crowd of fourth-class passengers, natives of all the east provinces of Africa, India, Arabia, and the many strange lands of the Orient, the scene was bizarre in the extreme. On one side in rudely constructed pens some half a dozen bony oxen lowed unhappily. Near them queerly shaped sheep, black of head and dingy white of body, bleated plaintively, while from their coops the pigeons, chickens, hens and roosters cooed, chirped, cackled and crowed dismally. The gaudily colored draperies of that wonderful assemblage of tropical and Eastern people lent a splendor of color to the small space. They spread out the gay mats and quilts that made their bedding, and establishing themselves thereon, settled down to enjoy the voyage, their simple cooking utensils at their elbows. Men and women smoked cigarettes, or chewed betel-nut or other delicacies, or thrummed little, silent mouth-organs. The women nursed their enchanting little brown or black babies, or discussed among themselves African fashions, or flirted most Orientally with the men, flashing brilliant teeth at them and exchanging chaff in rich, penetrating voices.

Within a few feet of these domestic and social scenes, which took place on the great, central hatchways, the ship's butcher would lead out the huge, slow, wide-horned ox. Planting it in the small open space permitted by the crowd, he would lift the heavy mallet and, with a great swing of his arm, fell the poor brute with a crashing blow. Generally a second and a third were necessary to still the convulsive quiverings. The black and brown races eyed the scene impassively, uncuriously. A small picaninny, nursing at his mother's breast, rolled his big eyes over his shoulders to take in the spectacle without removing his lips. The skinning, dissection and entire preparing of the animal took place then and there, and the carcass hung on the davits till the cook needed it. Do you wonder that I ate neither beef nor mutton on that trip?

Above, on the first-class deck, the passengers presented nearly as mixed an assemblage of nationalities as there was forward. English, Scotch, Irish, Germans, French, Portuguese, Italians and South Africans, all fraternized, while my mother and I were the only Americans on board. There were some little pet dogs that scampered about; also some monkeys, who occasionally escaped from their leashes or cages and rioted among us. A couple of suffering Portuguese infants filled the air with their wailings. The nurse who accompanied them on board, but would go no further, was a study in unique attire. He was black as the ace of spades, with an expression of severe dignity. He wore a high white collar, and white shirt, a neat black coat and waistcoat, and a bright red tie. But, in lieu of trousers, a crimson bandana handkerchief, spotted with black and white blobs, was tied about his waist, falling pretty far short of his knees, and was the only covering of his rather bandy legs. His place was taken by a little fat African boy of about twelve, who wandered about the ship clad in a ragged shirt and what might have been a dish-cloth about his waist. His method with the Portuguese infant, whom he carried in his arms all day, was to shake it up and down violently when it cried, which it did vigorously and frequently. I suppose it was somewhat on the principle of

> " Be gentle to your little boy
> And beat him when he sneezes.
> He only does it to annoy
> Because he knows it teases."

Like the baby in " Alice in Wonderland," this one looked as if it might turn into a pig at any moment.

SOME AFRICAN HIGHWAYS

At night the wretched African nurse curled up on the floor and went to sleep in any corridor where slumber happened to overtake him. He always looked the picture of woe. I do not think he got enough to eat, and I know his mistress was not kind to him and gave him many a blow. His large, heavy head, awkward body, and melancholy eyes left an unhappy memory.

As we steamed up the glassy stretches of the Indian Ocean with this motley boat-load, and, leaning on the ship's railing, I heard the speech of most of the civilized nations of Europe, mingling with the many African tongues from below, while dogs barked, monkeys jabbered, parrots screamed, oxen lowed, hens cackled, sheep bleated, and pigeons cooed, it seemed as if the ship were a travelling Berlitz School of Languages, with a barnyard attachment, or a second and more wonderful Noah's Ark. And, startled by our approach, flying-fishes sprang across the water in silver flashes by the myriad, or porpoises played about us, while in the harbors sharks floated around us, like pale, gray shadows waiting for the refuse from the kitchens, eying us greedily meanwhile.

And those tropical nights on deck — for the cabins were small and stuffy — shall I ever forget the silent stretches from midnight to dawn? The wind blew softly over the sea, the ship rose and fell on the long, slow swells, the stars glowed with a splendor we never see in the north. Silent forms were stretched out on mattresses laid on the deck, for most of the passengers preferred the open air to the closeness below. On the forward, lower deck a huddled mass of colored humanity, shrouded in strange draperies, wrapped in heavy slumber, lay still as the dead. Sleep touched me lightly, not as it does in my own downy couch. At the earliest streak of dawn on the eastern horizon I would wake up and watch the light strike the zenith and creep down to the wide horizon in soft splendor. On the lower decks the human bundles would unroll. Some would clean their teeth with split sticks. Others would gird themselves in their gorgeous draperies. The morning toilet of those on that lower deck was simple and interesting. In the steamer chairs near me dozing forms began to stir, though many slept until the sun was up. But these missed the gorgeous sunrises of the tropics, when sky and sea would be turned to gold and crimson, as the new day came with a leap.

At six o'clock early coffee, served on the decks, was partaken of with that informality which marks Oriental travel. Then the women descended to their cabins to get ready for the delicious salt bath which renews vigor in those latitudes, while the men stayed on deck to go through their exercises and morning walks before dressing. And thus began the ship's day.

Street in Zanzibar

Native Market in Zanzibar (Through Which Now Runs the Train)

CHAPTER XIII

MOZAMBIQUE TO ZANZIBAR

TO turn back on our tracks: Lorenco Marques lay sweltering in damp torridity behind us when we left Delagoa Bay about ten o'clock on a February morning. It was not until we were fairly under way in the Indian Ocean that we got rid of the sense of oppressive land heat, and could revel in the sea breezes which seldom fail on those broad stretches.

As we lay two nights later in the harbor at Beira — for there was nothing in this dreary spot to tempt one ashore — a strange chant, monotonous, rhythmical, apparently coming from the water and proceeding along the lower deck to the forward hatch, drew us to the overlooking front rail of our deck. There in the glare of the lights turned on the loading crews we saw one of the curious sights of an East

Coast trip: an ivory-bearing caravan bringing its load on board the ship. A line of turbaned men, each carrying on his right shoulder a huge elephant tusk, came up from a dhow lying alongside, and, keeping time to their own chant, marched to a small opening in the forward part of the ship, where they slid their loads down to some invisible recipient. We counted nearly fifty of these tusks, some so long and so heavy as to take two bearers. Their task done, the carriers united in a queer, shuffling dance, evidently a part of the performance. Probably their song recited the dangers of the chase which had yielded up this rich haul. Think of what getting this load of ivory meant; the many perils, the courage, brutality, skill, suffering and discomfort in dark jungles and savage wildernesses!

The only other incident of note at Beira was that we shipped as fellow passengers one of the most distinguished English generals, and also, that rather unusual combination, an Italian globe-trotter. These with a Scotch merchant from Singapore and his wife from

Glasgow, made up our table, and gave a wide variety to the talk. The dining-saloon was small, the food was atrociously bad, but through the ports one could see the moon shining on the sea, while from the lower forward deck came the muffled throb of a tom-tom accompanying a weird, minor crooning song from some of the fourth-class passengers, who seemed to be voicing all the despair of Africa. So *vogue la galere!* — who would not rather sail the tropical seas in the rottenest craft afloat than cross the Atlantic in the finest ocean greyhound?

It was afternoon when we glided into the harbor of Mozambique, rounding the point where the old fort rises from the green waters. A most picturesque and ancient landmark it is, having been built in fifteen hundred and something by the Portuguese, who were then the great navigators of the world, at the height of their power.

On our first visit to this port it had been too rough to land comfortably, so this time we gladly accepted the captain's offer to use the ship's pinnace and go ashore. The water-front of Mozambique is quite imposing, with a long, modern-looking pier running into the harbor, while a fine church, and some new red brick buildings front you on landing. These are flanked to the north by a pretty, green avenue of trees leading to the fort, and on the south by some picturesque cream, blue and pink houses. But, walking past the red buildings to the centre of the town — a dry, dusty, open square — brought us to a realizing sense of the utter deadness of the place. A few undersized Portuguese wandered listlessly about. An occasional native in long white gown, or girt in a bright print, sauntered idly by. The low, open shops displayed a hopeless array of granite ware, pots, canned goods and cheap calicoes. Oddly enough, connecting the East and the West by an unexplained link, in the centre of this principal *piazza* stood a bronze statue of the traditional North American Indian, while in a small adjacent open square was another of an Indian woman. There was no explanatory inscription on the pedestals, nor could our Portuguese fellow passengers give us any account of the inspiration of these civic ornaments. It was a silent reminder to us Americans of our debt to the remote Portuguese explorers.

It was weary work strolling about the neat, well-swept and deserted streets. There were none of the cheerful little kiosks which, in Lorenco Marques, give one a chance to sit down in the shade, or of the squalid saloons that send forth their alcoholic odors into the hot streets of Beira. Every shutter in every window in every house as far as the eye could reach was closed. The buildings were two-storied and of stucco construction, well preserved, in spite of the fact that two-thirds of them are said to be tenantless.

Discouraged by the silence and solitude, we turned away from the apathetic town and strolled out to the fort, the way leading us under some unknown trees that grew from the white sand, their gray-green, spiked leaves casting a pale, but grateful shade. Inside the courtyard at the fort the paved path led up to a very fine entrance with the Portuguese arms in richly carved stone over the gates. A friendly sentinel gave an air of intense animation to the scene by walking up and down almost briskly. It was a very paintable moment. Time has given the old fortress the mellowest, richest golden tones. Some gorgeous tropical shrubs flowered in the court. The waters of the bay glittered in the light of the setting sun. To the east, behind the fort, the Indian Ocean glared pale green, and dashed its white foam against encircling coral reefs. A native woman, in scant draperies of deep flame color, stood like a bronze statue, poising an earthenware water-jar on her head and watching us. It was the breathless moment between day and night when the wind is waiting new orders to blow. One felt the spirit of Africa, the dark, brooding genius of that vast, savage continent, rise from sand and sea and the low, distant mainland and assert itself, so that we were silent as we walked back to the pier. But our silence was most vigorously dispelled by the sight of the pinnace returning to the ship without us. It paid no heed to our cries and signals, so we supposed it would come back for us. We sat and waited. Overhead the dappled clouds turned to glowing crimson as the sun sank behind the distant palm groves. The lamps of the pier were lighted. The stars began to come out. A native, in flapping garments, needing a light for his cigarette, climbed one of the high posts to the pier lamps and amused us much by sticking his head into one of the glass globes to get at the flame.

A breath of hot air rose from the land and smote us, then a cool gust from the bay. But no one came from the ship to take us to our evening meal. The *cuisine*, which we had insulted the night before with opprobrious epithets, now seemed as alluring as Frederic's at La Tour d'Argent. Finally, in despair, we hailed a large, slow sloop and glided silently to the steamer's side. That we had been forgotten or overlooked made us both humble and hungry.

Dawn saw us heading for Zanzibar. We passed at rare intervals Arab dhows scudding along under their clumsy sails. It is not so very many moons since this whole coast was so infested with Arab slave-dealers that every dhow carried its quota of the dreadful trade. That it has been entirely stamped out is due to England's unremitting efforts and vigilance. But the traffic has left its mark on both crews and crafts, which look evil, furtive and menacing as they glide from port to port.

The island of Zanzibar lies between latitudes five and six south of the equator. It is noted as far back as 150 A. D. when the writings and maps of Ptolemy were produced. The best description of it, however, is given in an ancient work called " Periplus of the Erythraen Sea," in which, under the heading " A Pilot's Guide to the Indian Ocean," is an excellent account of the island. The history of Zanzibar, like that of Mombasa, is one of rapine, murder, and violence. Fierce African tribes, invading followers of Mahomet, marauding Portuguese, Turkish corsairs, have all in turn overrun, pillaged and ruled Zanzibar. The days of its prosperity began in 1890, when the English, by an exchange described in a previous chapter, got entire possession of the island, putting on the throne a new Sultan, and establishing order.

Zanzibar — the name was given by the Arabs and means " paradise " — is of coral construction, forty-seven miles long and twenty broad, with an area of 640 square miles. Low, undulating hills run north and south, reaching their greatest altitude, 800 feet, in the northern part of the island. The mean temperature is 80°. The hottest season is from January to March. The population of about 250,000 is composed of Arabs, Africans, Swahilis, Comoro Islanders, Parsees, Malagasies, Indians, and in fact representatives of all the races of Eastern Africa, Western Asia and Southern Europe.

The town of Zanzibar has about 60,000 inhabitants and is situated on the southwest shores of the long, low island. It is the principal port on the East Coast, though its harbor is little more than an open roadstead. Its chief exports are ivory, rubber, cloves, copra, ebony and gum copal. Nine-tenths of all the cloves used in the world are said to come from Zanzibar.

As the ship was to stay some two or three days in this harbor, we gladly accepted an invitation to spend that time under the roof of a hospitable English gentleman who was living in a quaint, old Arab house. The centre of the house was a great open court, the corridors and stairs of the first two or three floors gave on this court with wide arches, while our apartments at the top of the house looked down into it from one set of windows, while the opposite windows opened high above the narrow street. Indeed our room was open to all four points of the compass, so that, should any breeze blow, we should get it.

After a dinner, that by its excellence made us forget the ship's fare, we climbed many stairs to the roof. An Arab builder's idea of stairs is to have no contiguous two steps of the same height. This is unexpectedly disconcerting, but we reached the dizzy elevation above nevertheless, and revelled in the beauty of the night as we looked out over the town lying below us. To the west lay the harbor with the half a dozen ships riding at anchor there all alight. To the north, south and east stretched the roofs, walls, towers and minarets of the most picturesque place in East Africa. From the narrow winding ways below, the street lights sent up strange, fantastic shadows. A Mohammedan priest in a near-by mosque came out and, in full melodious voice, chanted the muezzin, or call to prayer. Many sounds rose muffled from the dimly lit city, while from the black dome above us the stars shone fiercely down, the moon not having yet risen. Late in the evening we all sallied forth, some in rickshaws, some on foot, to investigate the mysterious shadows of Zanzibar. We visited a most interesting house filled with rare treasures of the Orient from Japan to Egypt, and returned sated with strange impressions of shrouded forms, dark, mediæval streets, and silent, windowless dwellings.

Do your remember the Methodist minister's illustration of the warmth of the lower regions? " Brethren, have you ever seen the white hot metal in a foundry bubbling in the great caldrons? You know how it seethes and hisses there. Well — that is just *ice-cream* in Hell!" It would have been "just ice-cream" in Zanzibar at about six A. M. when the sun first came in over the roofs and minarets, and, slanting through the Venetian blinds, would not be denied. Breathless and gasping we turned and writhed on our beds. It was no use; sleep would not come again and that shaft of golden fire drove me up to sit in the windows on the west side of the room that overlooked a high-walled, Eastern garden, where rioted palms, ferns, and acacias, together with the gorgeous flamboyant and the blazing flame-of-the forest. Far below in the narrow, still shadowy street the throngs of tropical humanity were already astir, filling the air with a thick, incoherent murmur.

At seven the inevitable "boy," white-capped, white-robed and barefooted, came with his musical *hodi!* bringing in the tea and great platters of succulent fruit, pineapples, mangoes, pawpaws, bananas, Zanzibar oranges and others

Native Hut in Zanzibar

Zanzibar Fish Market

unknown. My favorite was the mango. A perfect mango is a rare treat. Those of Zanzibar were golden in color with red cheeks. To eat them you cut off a cheek and spoon out the juicy pulp, which has a delicious consistency and a flavor some say is turpentiny. It is quite an art to eat one gracefully. They are slippery and juicy, and prone to lead one into trouble. Furthermore they are not to be indulged in rashly. A little is good for one. Too much, however, brings on an unpleasant infliction known as mango boils. This was the only consideration that stayed me from entirely subsisting on mangoes.

The bath in the large, shallow tin tub had to be taken slowly, otherwise the deliciously cool water warmed one up too much. Breakfast at half-past eight — and such a good breakfast too! — was a pleasant meal. A boy in the corridor pulled the string which kept the punka going, and the great, high-ceilinged, bare room was so shady and cool that courage returned and nerved one to front the heat outside in a visit to the bazaars.

SOME AFRICAN HIGHWAYS

A quick run through shady, winding ways in rickshaws brought us to the street of the bazaars. There Indian merchants offered fascinating silver work, curious jewels, ivories, pongees, and embroidered silks from the East, also from Africa strange horns, canes made of rhinoceros horn, whips of the same, amber in hue, and many queer, native curios. Bargaining was necessary, in which the low-voiced gentle Oriental always got the better of his occidental customer. It was quite breathless outside, and the cool, dark shops, redolent with sandalwood and other spicy odors, were very pleasant. Our purchases completed, we were offered the invariable lime juice and water.

On our way home we passed shrouded vendors of jack-fruit, a huge, green, warty globe, first cousin to the durein-fruit. The latter is also to be found in Zanzibar, though I was unsuccessful in my quest. I was anxious to taste it, as it is considered a great delicacy by those who know it in the East Indies. It is described as having a fearful odor, like the rankest brie cheese, mixed with the strongest garlic, with a dash of kerosene. But those who partake of it become instantly oblivious to this. In the winding streets we met a certain strange, greasy smell which came out in hot puffs from low warehouses. This was the copra for which the island is famous. Copra is dried cocoanut and is used in the manufacture of oils and soaps. As the basis for stagnant air in a brassy heat, in narrow streets where black shade alternated with fervid glare, it is not to be overlooked or disregarded. Our ship carried away a large cargo of it, and for the rest of our trip northward we seldom were free from the permeating, sticky, oily, noisome odor. We woke up with it in our nostrils. We tasted it in our food. There were layers of it on the decks. To this day a latent bouquet in certain soaps calls up visions, with all the acute vividness which smells alone arouse, of that wretched ship, its crowded decks, its polyglot gathering of passengers, and its all-pervading reek.

CHAPTER XIV

A TRIP TO BU BU BU

HAVE you ever been to Bu Bu Bu? If not, do not call yourself a travelled person. Perhaps you do not even know where it is? Then do not make any claims to education. Bu Bu Bu is a settlement of low, straw huts in a shady grove of cocoanut-palms on the island of Zanzibar and is the terminus of a new and most important railroad, six and a half miles long, just completed, having been built by an American company. The company got the concession from the Sultan of Zanzibar. This same firm has also installed a new electric light plant which floods the Sultan's palace with a dazzling glare, while the same power-house keeps all the palace electric fans a-buzzing, much to the delight of the Zanzibar potentate. So the company is important. But it is an American concern.

Perhaps that was the reason the English residents did not like it. They based their right to object on the ground that the railroad runs through the principal street in the native quarter of the town. Zanzibar is so thickly built that there is no other outlet to the country than by this narrow, winding, truly wonderful highway. To get out otherwise would have meant tearing down hundreds of the human rabbit-hutches, which would have driven out thousands of that closely packed community. But this is not taken into consideration by the Britishers, who have brought all their influence to bear on the Sultan to revoke the license he gave the American company. He could not do this legally, unless they failed to keep their part of the contract to have the road in running order at a certain date. To accomplish this they started within the time specified one train a day to Bu Bu Bu. This daily mail left the sea-front at four P. M. Up till that hour of the day the building of the road was in active operation. Then any loose rails were hastily fastened down and the work discontinued till dawn the following day. To be sure the train often ran off these temporary rails, but there was no danger of collisions, as there was no other train on the island. Hard-pushed by his British subjects, the Sultan of Zanzibar, Ali bin Hamoud, at length threatened summarily to put in jail the perpetrators of this one and only railway in his dominions. This was during our stay, and as our host was hand in glove with the American offenders, and would have had to suffer with them, we were deeply interested in the struggle.

The possibility of seeing our genial friend at any moment marched off to a Zanzibar jail added a fearful spice to every-day life. But he and his confrères made the best of their resources. They suggested that they would cut off the lights and fan-power from the palace. This was too much for the Sultan, so he stayed his wrath. Personally he had a sneaking fondness for the enterprise. It added prestige to his kingdom. At any rate, when last heard of the trains were running, while the managers of the road were still at large, though not invited to social functions in the British colony.

Of course we went to Bu Bu Bu and with us went the distinguished English general, in spite of the fact that he was staying with the other faction, and that his host did not accompany him. It was a white-hot afternoon. The men and women of the party all wore white helmets and white linen suits, except the distinguished general, who wore a khaki helmet, a green suit and a scarlet tie.

He carried with him his sketch-book, his *vade mecum*. He is almost as noted for his pen and pencil as he is for his military achievements. He is an indefatigable worker and neither the heat of the tropics, nor unfavorable conditions could diminish his ardor. His little book was rich with very clever sketches taken *en route*. We rode through the narrow, dark streets in the light-rolling gharries and emerged suddenly into the blinding glare of the open sea-front where stood the little train.

This train was composed of a snorting, important little engine, one closed car with wicker chairs, and one open car with two seats back to back, running the length of the car. This latter was already packed with a chattering crowd of natives, to whom a ride on the new railway was the principal excitement of life. One solemn-visaged old Arab had made the trip every day since the road first opened. In the front car we found, besides the operators of the railway, two young cousins of the Sultan's, beautiful, sloe-eyed youths of twelve and fourteen, dressed in Eton suits, one wearing large diamond ear-rings in the upper part of the ears, while the other sported huge emeralds in the same fashion. They had gentle manners and soft voices. When I asked one how he was, he answered: " Thank you very much." It was his only phrase.

There was a tremendous clamor of voices, for a crowd always assembled for this daily departure. The engine shrieked in piercing fashion, its bell clanged, the white-gowned throng pulled each other excitedly off the tracks, the heat blazed up from the dazzling square, the perspiration rolled down our faces, for not a breath of air was stirring, and finally, with a plunge, the train rumbled slowly away. It turned almost immediately from the sea-front into one of the narrowest, queerest streets in the world. The foot-passengers flattened themselves against the walls of the low, plaster houses to let us by. From their little, shady porches men and women from every quarter of the Orient and tropics looked out at us in swarming thousands, chattering and gesticulating. The shrill whistle of the engine screamed frantically the whole of the time, filling the winding, close-packed way with a deafening din. Speech was impossible. We hung out of the windows in order not to lose a moment of the curious scene, with its gorgeous mingling of bright colors, strange types, fierce clamor and weird smells. Long before we reached the fish market we knew it was coming. There we saw sharks, swordfishes and many unknown kinds of sea-food hanging up or lying in odoriferous heaps on the steaming earth. When one realizes the way in which these people live one understands why bubonic plague is chronic in Zanzibar.

SOME AFRICAN HIGHWAYS

After we left this crowded quarter we ran near the sea. On the shore many camels paced across the sands with their haughty, melancholy tread, bearing loads of cocoanuts and cloves. We passed crumbling walls enclosing overgrown gardens full of tropical shrubs and trees, with perhaps here and there a seraglio peeping out of the depth of the dark foliage. It took us a little over an hour to traverse that six and a half miles. The road ended in a clay bank, up which we clambered, the native crowd dispersing in jabbering groups under the rattling palms. We sought an old Arab waterway, a straight channel of running water in ancient masonry, which burbled along through a delicious greenery composed of moss, ferns, acacias and palms. It was cool and shady and most exquisitely refreshing after the heat and glare. The land swarmed with black and brown people in gaudy colors or dazzling white. The sun was dropping in the west and glinted through tall, straight tree trunks. We visited one of the Sultan's summer palaces, a strange, forbidding structure, with a many-storied, dreary seraglio standing

Train for Bu Bu, Starting in Front of Sultan's Palace at Zanzibar

at the end of a bare court. A deep, dank, dark pool at one side of the palace, under black trees, suggested midnight drownings with muffled shrieks from heavy sacks.

The return trip was accomplished with the same clamor, excitement and confusion as the outgoing one, and the last crimson glow of sunset flooded the sea and land as we alighted from the train after one of the most thrilling railway journeys of my life.

That night we dined with the American perpetrator of the road, and his wife, who lived in a queer old Arab house. We mounted many steps, passed through large airy rooms furnished with richly carved teak-wood chairs, tables and screens, climbed still more stairs, and found ourselves on the dizzy heights of the roof with the dazzling canopy of the tropical night overhead. A breeze from the bay made the candles flicker. A huge Indian silver bowl, richly chased, holding some heavily scented unknown blossoms, stood in the middle of the table. On a still higher elevation of the roof the comfortable lounging-chairs that every Eastern household boasts invited us to rest, while the many servants padded noiselessly about, bringing cool drinks, and arranging to serve the dinner. Again we had the wonderful panorama of the city at our feet, and saw strange lights flickering up against white walls and minarets, and heard all the mysterious sounds blending and rising in a vast whisper to the stars. It is a rare treat thus to dine high above an Eastern city, with night winds just stirring the hot air and a sense of infinite space above and around one. The talk was delightful, the dinner delicious, and midnight came before we were once more in rickshaws on our way home, through the still and breathless streets. We passed shrouded forms sleeping along the way. A goat-herd with his flock lay all in heavy slumber in an angle of the road. A few ghostly wanderers, draped from head to foot in white, flitted noiselessly by, and copra and cloves, with an occasional whiff of sandalwood, tinged the night air.

The next day saw us on our way in our modern Noah's Ark to Dar Es Salaam, which we reached in time for afternoon tea on the cool, delightful terrace of the governor's house, overlooking the sea. The countess, the governor's wife, was holding her usual little court, and the scene, with its white pillars, Moorish arches, broad terraces and background of palms and baobabs and the blue Indian Ocean, was charming.

The drive which we took later led us under a long, straight double line of flamboyants (a semi-tropical tree), at that season all aflame with their gorgeous, trumpet-shaped, crimson blossoms. The setting sun gleaming across them made a glory of color I have never seen equalled.

The two nights that we spent at Dar Es Salaam we dined at the governor's, meeting each evening a most interesting circle of people; men who had achieved notable things out there, who had encountered danger in every form, and helped bring light into the Dark Continent; women who had borne the harder part of waiting on the edge of those vast solitudes for the men to come out of the wildernesses. One evening the dinner was served on the great, upper veranda, with the velvet curtain of the night as a background. The big, round table with its candles, garlands of flowers, glittering crystal and silver, and the encircling guests all in smartest of evening dress, made a brilliant oasis of color and light in that thick, enveloping, fragrant darkness.

The nights in the harbor were far from restful, for, preferring the greater coolness of the ship's deck, we did not accept the countess's hospitable invitation to stay with her. It was certainly cooler on the ship, but oh, so clamorously noisy! For, anxious to be on his way, the captain carried on his loading nearly all night. We were lashed to a steamer from India and Madagascar, and up till two in the morning, the engines and cranes filled the night with their din, interspersed with shouts and the exceeding vociferousness which attends all native labor. To stay in our cabins was out of the question, so we stretched ourselves on mattresses, or on long Bombay chairs, and dozed fitfully, never entirely losing consciousness of the strange lights and shadows thrown up from the busy, brilliantly lit, lower forward decks, or of the hoarse creakings, rattlings and shouts that rose from there. But a soft breath of air from the sea caressed us and we had none of the disease-bearing mosquitoes which infest the land. The deck-swabbing at five A. M. drove some below. I, however, preferred to tuck in my draperies and to get a final nap before the sun blazed in splendor across the rippling waters.

It was low tide when we steamed out of the landlocked harbor of Dar Es Salaam, and the waters had receded so far down the long, shiny beach to the narrow, winding, well-buoyed channel that the many natives who had waded out to the tide's edge to gather shell-fish seemed almost directly under the ship's side as we glided slowly along. They carried on their heads big baskets of loose weave and, with their scant, gay draperies and their glossy black skins, made a festival of color in the shallow, rippling waters. We took a last glance at the charming residency gleaming among the trees, and then the waving palms of Dar Es Salaam dropped from sight behind us, like many another lovely vision. We stopped at Zanzibar for a couple of hours to pick up the mails and some belated cargo, and then headed for Tanga.

It was sunset when we came into this harbor. To the left on a promontory stood the hospital, a fine building of cream-colored stucco with red tiled roof. Ahead of us a few other houses, half-hidden in foliage, indicated the town, which lay behind and away from the shore. It was night when we finally hailed a native and his boat and went to investigate the settlement. At the landing-place we found an evidence of German thoroughness, in a large board on which was written in German, English and French the proper boat fares. The pier was well lighted and everything was orderly and systematic. After leaving this cheerful spot, however, we plunged into Cimmerian darkness and stumbled along toward a far distant point of light, until we bumped into the ship's baggage-master, who told us that a little further on we would find one of those delightful hand-trolleys which so often solve the problem of transportation in East Africa. Having seated ourselves in one, our troubles were over and we flew through the delicious, thick, fragrant night until we found ourselves in the comparative glare of the main corner in Tanga. We indicated in our best Swahili that we wished to go on and see more, so our barefooted, white-frocked human steed rushed us along broad, shaded highways where, on either side, lights shone out from low door-ways. We stopped at some and went into stuffy interiors inhabited by natives or Indians selling various commodities. We pulled out the gaudy prints which they use for dresses and made a selection. We offered for two of these the price which they asked for one and the offer was promptly accepted. A pale light from a paraffine lamp overhead illumined the dingy interior. A straight-haired Goanese made the sale, while a stalwart and ill-smelling African rather sullenly hauled the things out for us. It was a relief to be out once more in the sweet-smelling blackness of the shaded roads. Through the leaves we could get glimpses of fierce stars.

We halted again at the Botanical Gardens. Winding paths, tall palms, giant ferns all lured us into the darkest, quietest place I ever felt; for we could see nothing when the matches we lit went out. It is amazing, however, the feeling of security we had in that utterly remote, unexplored place. The night held no terrors for us. It was more orderly and law-abiding than most modern cities are after sunset. And it is curious that this should be so, for after all these swarming natives are only one remove from savages. Occasionally some isolated tragedy occurs, like the case of Harry Galt, which shakes the sense of security that grows up among the handful of whites who live in and rule over these vast and thickly populated territories in the Dark Continent.

We found our way back to shore and there secured a boat to take us to the ship, which was a quarter of a mile or so away across the glassy, black water. Morning saw us at sea again headed for Mombasa.

CHAPTER XV

THE LAST OF THE TROPICS

FOR the third time we came to Mombasa. The hottest of the hot seasor. was in full sway. The mango-trees that line the charming highway from Kilindini, on the west side of the island, to Mombasa on the east, cast a blacker shade on the white coral sand road. All the many colors that dazzled us on our first visit there seemed even more intense now. I can give only a small idea of the utterly tropical effect of the low grass huts under the rattling palms; of the swarming throngs of chattering black and brown people who seem as much a part of the place as the trees and flowers; of the strangely pungent or oppressively sweet odors that came in hot gusts from either side of the way; of the glimpses of indigo sea, and of the overarching deep blue sky where rode that terrible

313

source of heat and light that seems only a distant cousin to the milder sun of the temperate zones.

While the sun of the tropics is so dangerous it is at the same time the great salvation of those regions, the chief sanitary agent, destroying microbes and all disease-breeding refuse. They say there that ten minutes' exposure to the sun's rays of any article infected with smallpox germs purifies it entirely. Even the insect world is helpless in contact with these rays. A box of lump sugar, having been invaded by the small, red ants which swarm over everything there, was laid out on a sheet of paper in the sun. In twenty minutes there was not an ant left except some little, blackened corpses of those that had lingered too long. They could not stand the fierce heat.

It is most dangerous for a European to go even for a few minutes with the head uncovered, exposed to the sun's rays. The longer you live there the more do you realize this. The pith helmet is the safest head-covering, while it is advisable to have all parasols interlined with dark green if possible.

THE LAST OF THE TROPICS

The natives, however, do not seem to suffer from the direct rays. *Sans* head-covering they toil all day with no ill effects.

Once more we ran in the little rumbling trolleys over the shining rails across the island, and found ourselves in the queer, old streets of the town. At one corner of the main street stood the ancient, windowless tower of a mosque, looking like a white plaster pepper-pot. The old houses of Mombasa all butt into the street, each at its own angle. Many of the doorways are fine specimens of carving, the teak-wood jambs and lintels being wrought into strange, Oriental designs. There is much coming and going of white-gowned Indians and gaudily draped Africans As they push the trains of heavily laden trucks on the narrow tracks, the almost naked natives sing a wailing, minor chant with a marked rhythm that is strangely thrilling — one of the finest effects of sound I ever heard. It rings in my ears still, though months and leagues intervene since I last heard it rising and swelling with heart-breaking melancholy, its undertones of deep, accented guttural notes sounding like the march in perfect unison of thousands of bare feet.

The night of our arrival we dined at Judge H——'s, where we had dined our first evening on African soil. It was too warm to endure any covering over our shoulders, so, bareheaded and bare-necked, we descended the ship's side, got into a small boat, and were rowed across the black, lapping waters. We climbed the high bank and found the distinguished English general, who had left the ship at Mombasa, ready to escort us. A white-gowned boy was also there with a lantern to light us to the trolley a quarter of a mile away in a mango grove. We stumbled along the sandy trail, the lantern twinkling in the thick darkness, lighting up the coarse, sparse grass and the many creeping things that scuttled away at our coming. Some frangipani, unseen but perceptible, scented the still, heavy air. We saw a distant spark of light; it was the lantern of the little trolley that waited for us in a hollow. We were glad to find ourselves sitting in it and rushing swiftly through the night. The wind of our passage

316

cooled our overheated faces. It was fascinating going through the utterly silent, oppressively heavy blackness of that tropical evening. Used as we are to the gentle and lingering twilights of the temperate zones, the practically unvarying twelve hours of darkness of the equator was a never-failing sensation.

The dinner was delightful, and the return to the ship even more curious in the accompanying impressions of solitude, silence, and impenetrable mysterious night. Through this we two little, lonely American women were speeding, this time without escort, bareheaded, bare-shouldered, in very nice silk evening costumes, peopling the palpable dark, as we went, with horrid tropical phantoms. " What agonies we undergo for things that never happen after all! " Quite safely we climbed the steps swinging on the ship's side and made our way to our cabins at midnight.

The next day's hot noon saw us on our way out to the cool stretches of the Indian Ocean. We had shipped as passengers here an Italian family from Mogadisho, a sacred city situated on the dreariest stretch of East African sea-shore, a little north of the equator. They had brought with them an Arab boy and a Madagascar monkey. The former was a handsome lad of about ten or twelve, who wore the most enchanting turbans of magenta and blue, and picturesque gowns of many stripes and colors. His charge, the monkey, was a beautiful little creature, of softest fur, striped black and white, big, prominent brown eyes, and a long and very wonderful tail, ringed black and white. These two, when we came to the chill of the Red Sea, shrivelled up and, wrapped in the folds of a heavy Scotch travelling-cape, all that was visible were two little pinched faces peering reproachfully at the world. We all felt the cold when the thermometer dropped below 70° and the wintry winds blew from the fierce, bleak mountains that rim the Arabian desert.

At Aden we drove up to see the tanks, a disappointing spectacle, though the drive was interesting, passing as it does through a narrow gorge of red, overhanging rocks, and coming out on a flat, sandy, glaring stretch, where the low, plaster houses seem like mere excrescences. We passed caravans of camels, looking shabby and moth-eaten, and bearing loads of coffee from that mysterious interior country that so few Europeans have penetrated.

At Aden Asia and Africa touch and present the most wonderful mingling of strange human types to be seen anywhere. The ship was surrounded with small boats filled with clamoring hordes wishing to sell all sorts of things: ostrich feathers in every shape and color; beautiful baskets of native make; many kinds of ivory and silver work; strange sea products; and scarves and draperies of every variety. The people who offered the things were even more curious and interesting than their wares. Queer, greasy-looking Asiatic Jews, wearing conical shaped caps, with long shiny ringlets oozing forth in front of their ears, with high hooked noses and scraggly beards, came pawing our sleeves and fawningly striving to attract our attention to their stock of feathers; a rascally untrustworthy lot they were! Little semi-nude Arab boys tried to make us buy a primitive native tooth-brush, a stick split at the end, which they first energetically used to polish their own brilliantly gleaming teeth, and then vociferously offered to us. Every race and race-mixture clamored and swarmed about the sides of the ships in the fierce glare of the noon sun. Those passengers who did not care to meet them on the deck hung out of their ports and bargained with the merchants in small boats, purchases being pulled up by strings, and money let down in the same way. It was a most amusing sight. The big empty coal-barges with their crews, red-headed, black-skinned and naked, lay off at a little distance. The town gleamed white across the glittering waters against its background of brutally bare crimson rocks. All was an orgy of fierce color, light and din. It was our last glimpse of the East and the tropics. I shall long remember it.

It grew quite cold as we steamed northward to the Suez Canal. A wintry blast from the Mediterranean swept down across the isthmus. At Suez, as we lay awaiting our turn to enter the canal, while we were looking at the town, the sand from the desert seemed to rise in one mighty cloud and blot out earth and sky and sea. Our ship swung heavily around on its anchor, as the dry blast struck us; the decks became covered with gritty dust, and we had a slight taste of one of the celebrated sand-storms of Sahara.

The wind had not died down when we reached Port Said, and the wide streets of that city were filled with spirals of sand and dead leaves, whirling up and down like dancing dervishes. We browsed around in the excellent shops here, and had some very good tea and English pound-cake in a pleasant, sunny, upper parlor of a hotel. The ship's fare had not improved with the passing weeks, though by this time we had eaten up our entertaining and musical barn-yard and were subsisting on what the cook bought at the various ports.

A lively blow in the Mediterranean greeted us as we left the canal. With slight intermission this kept up the four and a half days it took us to reach Naples, though the morning was a brilliant one when we steamed through the straits of Messina. To the right lay the bold promontories and quaint towns of Calabria. To the left Ætna, still snow-topped, overhung everything in Sicily. We saw Taormina the beautiful, gleaming half-way up the charming hillside to which it clings, and we noted many other landmarks. Stromboli, when we passed it, was enveloped in its own smoke, which shrouded it like a heavy mantle. Vesuvius looked rather pensive as we entered the Bay of Naples, though that night from our hotel windows we saw two glowing streams of lava, like deep gashes in its hoary sides, but nothing to indicate the catastrophe that was imminent.

Having met lions face to face in East Africa and a sand-storm at Suez, it remained for us to go through the most terrific Vesuvian eruption since 1631 to fill our cup of experiences and sensations full to the brim.

CHAPTER XVI

OUR FINAL EXCITEMENT

ON Wednesday, April 4th, as I was returning from a day in charming Capri, I noticed that the throng of tourists that daily crowded the Capri steamers were all looking at Vesuvius with unusual excitement, and, turning, I saw a thick coil of brown smoke oozing out of the crater, quite different from the usual intermittent puffs. It rose a little way and then was blown in a long, slow stream out across the bay, and soon a shower of fine cinders fell on us as we sat looking up at the mountain. This was the beginning of the great eruption of 1906.

For three days the smoke poured forth in constantly increasing volume. The wind had changed, sending this north and westwards, so that at night, what was a splendid spectacle from Castellamare and Sorrento, could not be

323

seen from Naples. But we occasionally heard sounds like the boom of distant cannon from the mountain, while the sun glared dimly through the yellow haze, and each morning on our balcony the deposit of volcanic dust was heavier. Still we felt no fear, nor thought that it was other than one of the fine eruptions with which Vesuvius is wont to entertain the surrounding country. By Saturday, however, the explosions became louder and more frequent, the discharge of smoke and ashes heavier, and crowds began to gather in the streets and on housetops, looking toward the mountain and wondering what was going to happen. There was a feeling of not unpleasant excitement in the air; the timid could be heard complaining. Reports from the other side of the mountain said that a large and fresh stream of lava was creeping down the eastern flanks and menacing vineyards and the small and thickly settled towns that clung in fancied security to the great chimney. The fumes and clouds of smoke grew thicker. The cinders, that fell still lightly on our faces, tasted salty and sulphurous, made our eyes smart, and irritated our throats. People began to wear veils, masks or goggles. That night the reverberations grew louder; the sense of an imminent something became oppressive. A large percentage of the travelling public who were then gathered in Naples notified the hotel-keepers that they would go to Rome the next morning, and spent the evening packing. Others, more adventurous, had gone to Castellamare, whence the spectacle was one of fearful splendor. At two o'clock in the morning two appalling reports in quick succession shook the town and fairly knocked me out of bed. The mountain had blown out two new craters near the summit on the southeast side. The ashes were falling so fast that the city lights were dim. The next morning came terrifying reports of the destructions on the east flank. A stream of lava forty feet high and a thousand feet broad had moved at a stately pace and with irresistible force down through vineyards and olive groves, overwhelming the town of Bosco-Tre-Case and menacing Torre Annunziata on the sea. Many from Naples had spent the night on the eastern slope watching the wonderful and terrible sight. The Duke of Aosta was there at the head of the troops helping the people to escape, forcing many of them to leave their doomed houses; for, in spite of the showers of molten stones, the fierce detonations, and the sight of the slowly on-creeping lava, many refused to believe in danger, and, when they clung to their miserable hovels, had to be dragged away by force.

Sunday afternoon all of Naples was taking vehicles and trams out to the base of the mountain to get a near view of the eruption. With great difficulty we secured a cab and drove out in that direction. The streets of the lower part of the city were already filled with wandering crowds of refugees carrying pitiful loads of bedding and clothing, old women and young children being helped along by the rest. As a rule they were silent, seeming dazed by the catastrophe, but occasionally loud wails would rise and all the passers-by would shake their heads and murmur, " *Poverini!* "

OUR FINAL EXCITEMENT

The way to the foot of the mountain was thronged with two streams of vehicles going in opposite directions, one carrying excited, chattering Neapolitans out to see the show, the other bringing in, on piles of household goods, the wretched peasants, who had been driven forth by their mother, the mountain. They looked silently and reproachfully at the eastward hurrying band, to whom their misfortune was merely an entertaining spectacle.

When we got as far as Resina, which is built above the site of Herculaneum, we turned into a little open square whence we had an uninterrupted view of the mountain from its base to its terrible summit. The ground under us shook with the internal rumblings. The crater had crumbled so that its awful mouth was twice its ordinary width and from this rose to the zenith the majestic pillar of smoke and fire, shot with lightning. At the top it spread out into the dreaded pine-tree shape which always means mischief. Nothing was ever more awfully beautiful than this column of constantly changing color, with the fumes writhing and bubbling into wonderful, soft, thick puffs of smoke. Every now and then loud explosions rent the air and gorgeous electrical displays would zig-zag through the dun colored mass.

On our way to town we had to draw up on one side to let the soldiers press back the throngs of wretched refugees who sought to return to their devastated homes. We saw many others preparing to camp by the roadside, spreading out bedding and getting ready their food. The poor people who lived along the road brought out of their slender store things for the refugees. All the wayside shrines were lit as we drove back and many people were kneeling in front of them with bowed heads, praying aloud for mercy and pity.

That night the fall of ashes became so thick that the lights of the city below us were entirely blotted out. Even the one across the street from our hotel was only faintly visible. It was like gazing into the depth of a Dakota blizzard to look out that night at Naples. And with the falling ashes fell a great silence. The volcanic dust lay so thick as to muffle all sounds of wheels or hoofs and to strangle all street or city noises.

It was still falling the next morning, hiding the sun and the light of day. On the Chiaia and the Toledo, the two principal streets, the lights burned all day. Many shops were closed. Most of the factories stopped work, and the people on the streets carried umbrellas, while many wore masks to protect them from the distressing ashes. Every leaf, every blossom, every blade of grass was coated with the dun colored dust. The once beautiful palms and ilexes of the public gardens looked like trees in a petrified forest. The same drab hue covered the pink, yellow and blue palazzi that used to give such a gay effect to Naples.

And still the ashes fell. The city by this time was nearly empty of the tourists who had been bringing their annual harvest to the hotels.

Monday afternoon I again drove out to the foot of the mountain. This time the road was a foot deep in ashes. In some places a volcanic rain had fallen and changed them to black mud which lay in thick masses many feet in height along the side of the way, as the people were clearing their roofs as fast as they could, the unwonted weight threatening every house. By the time we got to Resina the road had become almost impassable. The horses plowed through it, breathing heavily. The coachman got down and said that he could go no farther. At that moment a sudden darkness descended on us and out of the darkness fell a terrific shower of hot water and mud. The Italians near us became terrified. The driver besought us, with tears streaming down his face, to return. We were not ready yet; we had seen nothing but darkness, ashes and frightened people, so we told him to get under shelter, and we started to walk up the mountainside. We soon passed out from under the volcanic shower and emerged in the clearer space directly below the dreadful cone. Every sprig of vegetation in the fields about us had been killed and covered by the ashes. The desolation was complete. And above us Vesuvius belched forth that fearful column of smoke and fire —

which rose, scientists who were on the spot said, to the height of six miles. It was irresistibly fascinating to watch the convolutions of the writhing smoke spirals, thick and of an angry gray hue, with every now and then a puff of white steam like a bursting bomb. The detonations were not so loud as on the previous day, but the mountain-sides still trembled with suppressed fury, and the discharge of volcanic matter was much greater. By this time the ashen walls of the crater had entirely crumbled away, and the mouth yawned across the whole summit. Any personal emotion like fear was lost in a certain awful ecstasy inspired by the spectacle. Human insignificance is a wholesome realization.

The drive back to the city was slow and distressing, through darkness, with alternating showers of ashes and mud making the road almost impassable for the poor, laboring horses. On the way the king and some of his officers passed us in an automobile. The whole party was so covered with mud and volcanic dust that it was hard to recognize them.

That night and often through the following days we saw dreary little processions of people in the streets carrying candles and sacred images, and chanting prayers, as they walked from church to church through the softly falling ashes. Everywhere every one spoke to every one else in the common brotherhood created by a great catastrophe.

The sand and mud storm, of which we got merely the outer edge, destroyed the towns of Ottaiano and San Giuseppe. In the latter place, as the people, distraught by fear, rushed into the streets, the priest called them all to come to the church to pray for mercy. Several hundred were gathered there when the roof fell under the weight of stones and mud, and two hundred were killed or fatally injured. Altogether I believe that more people perished in this eruption of Vesuvius than in the San Francisco disaster.

The usual morning throng was collected in the covered market-place at Naples on the first Tuesday of the eruption when the great girders supporting the roof gave way, with a grinding crash and roar, and, coming down, buried scores in the ruins. The number of those killed and wounded here went up into the hundreds.

Some Americans who were to sail for home early Tuesday morning sent all their luggage on board the preceding afternoon. When they went down in the evening to embark on the ship, which lay out in the harbor, the officers of the tender refused to take them, as the ashes were falling so thickly that everything was enveloped in darkness, and it would have been impossible to find the ship. They were obliged to return to the hotel minus even hand-luggage and wait a week for the next boat, all their belongings going to America without them.

Each day we looked out in the morning for some signs of let up in the dreary and depressing fall of ashes. On the Thursday, nine days after the beginning of the eruption, the air was still so thick with them, as we drove along the Chiaia, that it felt like snow beating against our faces, while the brown shower lying on everything and everybody took away all differences of appearance, making the prince look like the

pauper. One of the most disagreeable of the
minor features of those ashen days was that it
was impossible to keep the hair free from these
volcanic cinders. In spite of many enveloping
veils it became so permeated that the daily
dressing was like dragging the comb through a
sand pile. Each hair was coated with the im-
palpable dust and gritted audibly. All vitality
and gloss and color, even, disappeared. Of
course the ashes ruined clothes and shoes.

And still the dreadful shower continued.
The first fall was a pale gray in color. Then
it changed to a dark, almost black hue, and the
latter days a dun brown ash fell. All these
indicated the different strata that the mountain
was throwing up, the last being evidently iron,
as both color and weight indicated, a handful
being noticeably heavy. The first gray fall
was pumice stone and was excellent stuff for
polishing brass and silver.

Meanwhile the city officials, the army, the
clergy and members of the royal family all
worked day and night to rescue and succor
the sufferers. There were many unrecorded

deeds of heroism, and many tales of distress and danger. The wretched dwellers on the mountain-sides not only lost their homes but also the use of their land for a generation. It is said that, though ultimately of fertile effect, it takes this volcanic dust thirty years or so to amalgamate thoroughly with the soil on which it falls.

We went one day to Torre Annunziata to see the place where the mighty flood of lava had stopped just at the door of a church. Here a miracle had been wrought. The image of the Virgin in this church had been carried to the edge of the on-coming torrent. The latter had paused in its course, and then turning, plunged down the valley to the left, leaving the church and its little encircling cemetery unharmed, though the statue was somewhat singed.

It was quite an awful sight, that volcanic torrent forty feet high and a thousand feet broad. A huge and ancient stone pine, caught in the flood, was tossed high to the top of the stream, singed to a black crisp. Along the course of the torrent stood houses cut in two, as if with a knife, revealing pathetic interiors. One on the edge showed a section of an upper room with a crimson sofa tipping on the sloping floor. Pictures still hung all awry on the walls and curtains flapped at the windows. The lower part of the house was flooded with the lava, now cooled off and black.

At length we grew weary of waiting for the mountain to subside. Like many things and many people it didn't seem to know when to stop. It kept on long after all novelty was passed. It became tiresome, monotonous; we began to talk of other things; we grew used to the twilit days, the falling ashes, the thick clouds of smoke, the muffled sounds, the deserted hotels, to the vision as of a dead city. We began to long for sunshine and normal sensations, so finally, on Easter Sunday, we went to Capri, where from our balconies, across a lavender carpet of wistaria in fullest bloom, we could look over the sea to the terrible and still belching mountain.

Spring was at its loveliest there, and, as we sat in the warm and fragrant sunlight, on those

charming terraces and saw the ships pass by
from all the ports in the world (though it was
those from Africa we gazed at longest) we took
time to marshal our many memories of strange
lands; and to realize that the wonderful journey
to which we had so long looked forward, for
which we had so long planned, which we had so
intensely enjoyed, was now in the past, a thing
of dreams, a fulfilled realization.

CHAPTER XVII

A WORD OF COUNSEL

FOR those who wish to make one of the most interesting trips in the world and visit a strange and wonderful continent, I will give some information and a few suggestions as to the routes and best way and time to make the journey.

Although England has such large interests on the East Coast of Africa, she has no first-class line of steamers touching at the ports there. The three lines which carry most of the passenger service are the Austrian Lloyd,[1] sailing from Trieste, the Messagerie Maritime from Marseilles, and the German East African Line from Hamburg, touching at such Mediterranean ports as Marseilles, Genoa, and Naples. The Austrian Lloyd boats are the favorite with

[1] Since writing the above the service of this line has been discontinued.

the British officials on the East Coast. Of the
Messagerie boats I know little except that they
undoubtedly have an excellent table. Of the
German East African Line, on which I have
travelled three times, I can only say that they
have the advantages and defects of German
lines the world over. You always feel safe on a
German ship — even if you do have veal and
pork served in the Red Sea with the thermometer hovering near the hundred mark. This
line makes the entire circuit of Africa. Do you
realize that Africa is the only continent which
can be entirely circumnavigated by the ordinary
traveller? You can sail from Hamburg, either
going down the West Coast and returning by
the East Coast, or vice versa, a trip which takes
about three months. The larger ships on this
line are very comfortable. The smaller ones
are to be avoided. You will need rather a large
and assorted wardrobe to make the journey
comfortably, but as you have access to the
luggage-room on certain days of the week, this
is easily arranged. A useful dress for women
is a thin, unlined silk or cotton costume of

black and white check, or dark blue, as at times of coaling the ship is apt to get very dirty. This should be supplemented by light summer dresses and some pretty frocks to be worn in the evenings. For men a khaki suit and a few white linen suits are desirable, in addition to an ordinary outfit.

As the southeast monsoon blows from June to the end of September, it is not advisable to take the trip down the East Coast at that season. Rough seas are unavoidable, and as the heat, especially in the Red Sea, is apt to be intense, the fact that ports have to be kept closed makes life below decks unendurable, even for good sailors.

The most interesting part of the whole journey is the trip on the Uganda Railway up to the lake and on the steamer either crossing the lake or making the ten days' tour of the lake. The traveller can break his passage on the coast and wait a month for the next boat. This month can be well spent at Mombasa, Nairobi and Entebbe. From Nairobi expeditions can be made into the surrounding country, where excellent shooting and hunting can be had. From Entebbe most interesting journeys may be made into the interior. The month will pass all too quickly.

The other ports on the way south can be sufficiently seen in the days the steamer spends in unloading and taking on cargo.

From Beira one can go up by rail and take in Salisbury, Rhodesia, and the great Victoria Falls, the pride of Great Britain, one of the magnificent spectacles of the world. According to report, these falls have quite put out of joint the nose of our beautiful Niagara. From Salisbury the traveller can go by the Cape to Cairo, railway to Pretoria and Johannesburg, and thence can catch his steamer either at Durban or at Cape Town. Or else, if he does not care to make this détour to the Zambesi, which at certain seasons of the year is an unpleasant trip, owing to drought and dust, he can stay on his ship until he arrives at Delagoa Bay, whence he can, by train, in twenty-four hours, reach Johannesburg. From there, after he has seen the mines and Pretoria (which lies a couple of hours away) he can go to Durban and see, *en route*, Natal — called " the garden of South Africa " — and even stop a few hours in Pietermaritzburg, the capital of Natal, before rejoining his ship *en route* to the Cape. On the way to Cape Town two pretty harbors and towns are visited, East London and Port Elizabeth.

Table Bay, as the harbor of Cape Town is called, is one of the most beautiful harbors in the world. Flat-topped Table Mountain, leaning over the city with massive, frowning ramparts, is very impressive. The whole bay is ringed with mountains and hills vying in lovely tints with those of Southern Italy, while the waters of the harbor reflect the tints of sky and shore.

If the visitor to South Africa prefers to take in Kimberly and the diamond mines to seeing the coast towns, he can go there by rail, and thence to Cape Town, crossing the Karoo Desert. This is in case he is travelling by the German line. The Austrian and French boats only go to Durban, and then retrace their steps up the East Coast to their respective starting-points, Trieste and Marseilles.

The German boats on their way up the West

Exchange Building at Johannesburg

Coast stop at Swakopmund, the port of German Southwest Africa, and at Madeira.

At every port in landing you can find porters, guides, and interpreters. Also hotels — though one must not expect to find these hostelries like the Waldorf-Astoria, Carlton or Ritz. Of the two principal ones in Mombasa it is said that if you go to one you always wish you had gone to the other. There are excellent hotels in all the South African cities, and travel there is in every way most comfortable, and not as expensive as in America.

With a reasonable amount of care and a not necessarily large bank account, you can make, with safety and comfort, one of the most delightfully interesting voyages in the world. But certain things you must have. First and foremost, good health — secondly, an open mind, free from prejudices — thirdly, a willingness to make light of trifles and to put up with small discomforts. Only thus equipped can you get the full joy and benefit of this great journey.

THE END.

African River Steamer-landing

Featured Titles from Westphalia Press

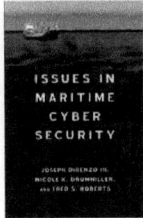

Issues in Maritime Cyber Security Edited by Nicole K. Drumhiller, Fred S. Roberts, Joseph DiRenzo III and Fred S. Roberts

While there is literature about the maritime transportation system, and about cyber security, to date there is very little literature on this converging area. This pioneering book is beneficial to a variety of audiences looking at risk analysis, national security, cyber threats, or maritime policy.

The Rise of the Book Plate: An Exemplative of the Art by W. G. Bowdoin, Introduction by Henry Blackwel

Bookplates were made to denote ownership and hopefully steer the volume back to the rightful shelf if borrowed. They often contained highly stylized writing, drawings, coat of arms, badges or other images of interest to the owner.

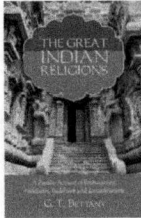

The Great Indian Religions by G. T. Bettany

G. T. (George Thomas) Bettany (1850-1891) was born and educated in England, attending Gonville and Caius College in Cambridge University, studying medicine and the natural sciences. This book is his account of Brahmanism, Hinduism, Buddhism, and Zoroastrianism

Unworkable Conservatism: Small Government, Freemarkets, and Impracticality by Max J. Skidmore

Unworkable Conservatism looks at what passes these days for "conservative" principles—small government, low taxes, minimal regulation—and demonstrates that they are not feasible under modern conditions.

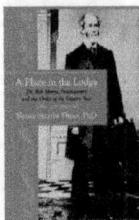

A Place in the Lodge: Dr. Rob Morris, Freemasonry and the Order of the Eastern Star by Nancy Stearns Theiss PhD

Ridiculed as "petticoat masonry," critics of the Order of the Eastern Star did not deter Rob Morris' goal to establish a Masonic organization that included women as members. As Rob Morris (1818-1888) came "into the light," he donned his Masonic apron and carried the ideals of Freemasonry through a despairing time of American history.

Demand the Impossible: Essays in History as Activism
Edited by Nathan Wuertenberg and William Horne

Demand the Impossible asks scholars what they can do to help solve present-day crises. The twelve essays in this volume draw inspiration from present-day activists. They examine the role of history in shaping ongoing debates over monuments, racism, clean energy, health care, poverty, and the Democratic Party.

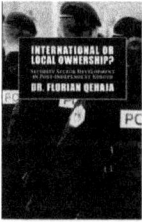

International or Local Ownership?: Security Sector Development in Post-Independent Kosovo
by Dr. Florian Qehaja

International or Local Ownership? contributes to the debate on the concept of local ownership in post-conflict settings, and discussions on international relations, peacebuilding, security and development studies.

The Bahai Movement: A Series of Nineteen Papers
by Charles Mason Remey

Charles Mason Remey (1874-1974) was the son of Admiral George Collier Remey and grew up in Washington DC. He studied to be an architect at Cornell (1893-1896) and the Ecole des Beaux Arts in Paris (1896-1903), where he learned about the Baha'i faith, and quickly adopted it.

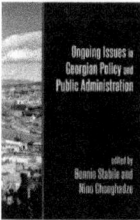

Ongoing Issues in Georgian Policy and Public Administration
Edited by Bonnie Stabile and Nino Ghonghadze

Thriving democracy and representative government depend upon a well functioning civil service, rich civic life and economic success. Georgia has been considered a top performer among countries in South Eastern Europe seeking to establish themselves in the post-Soviet era.

Poverty in America: Urban and Rural Inequality and Deprivation in the 21st Century
Edited by Max J. Skidmore

Poverty in America too often goes unnoticed, and disregarded. This perhaps results from America's general level of prosperity along with a fairly widespread notion that conditions inevitably are better in the USA than elsewhere. Political rhetoric frequently enforces such an erroneous notion.

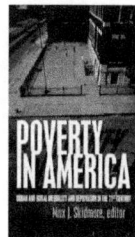

westphaliapress.org

www.ingramcontent.com/pod-product-compliance
Lightning Source LLC
La Vergne TN
LVHW051252080426
835509LV00020B/2933